START YOUR OWN

FOOD TRUCK BUSINESS

Second Edition

D0817449

Additional titles in *Entrepreneur's* Startup Series

Start Your Own

Arts and Crafts Business

Automobile Detailing Business

Bar and Club

Bed and Breakfast

Blogging Business

Business on eBay

Car Wash

Child-Care Service

Cleaning Service

Clothing Store and More

Coaching Business

Coin-Operated Laundry

College Planning Consultant Business

Construction and Contracting Business

Consulting Business

Day Spa and More

eBusiness

Event Planning Business

Executive Recruiting Business

Fashion Accessories Business

Florist Shop and Other Floral Businesses

Food Truck Business

Freelance Writing Business and More

Freight Brokerage Business

Gift Basket Business and More

Grant-Writing Business

Graphic Design Business

Green Business

Hair Salon and Day Spa

Home Inspection Service

Import/Export Business

Information Marketing Business

Kid-Focused Business

Lawn Care or Landscaping Business

Mail Order Business

Medical Claims Billing Service

Net Services Business

Nonprofit Organization

Online Coupon or Daily Deal Business

Online Education Business

Personal Concierge Service

Personal Training Business

Pet Business and More

Pet-Sitting Business and More

Photography Business

Public Relations Business

Restaurant and More

Retail Business and More

Self-Publishing Business

Seminar Production Business

Senior Services Business

Staffing Service

Travel Business and More

Tutoring and Test Prep Business

Vending Business

Wedding Consultant Business

Wholesale Distribution Business

Entrepreneur.
MAGAZINE'S

STARTUP

START YOUR OWN

FOOD TRUCK BUSINESS

Second Edition

CART · TRAILER · KIOSK
STANDARD AND GOURMET TRUCKS
MOBILE CATERING · BUSTAURANT

The Staff of Entrepreneur Media, Inc. & Rich Mintzer

Ep
Entrepreneur
PRESS®

Entrepreneur Press, Publisher
Cover Design: Andrew Welyczko
Production and Composition: Eliot House Productions

This publication is designed to provide accurate and authoritative information in regard to the subject matter covered. It is sold with the understanding that the publisher is not engaged in rendering legal, accounting or other professional services. If legal advice or other expert assistance is required, the services of a competent professional person should be sought.

Library of Congress Cataloging-in-Publication Data
    Start your own food truck business/by The Staff of Entrepreneur Media, Inc. and Rich Mintzer.—Second edition.
        pages cm.—(Startup series)
        Includes index.
        ISBN-13: 978-1-59918-564-4 (alk. paper)
        ISBN-10: 1-59918-564-4 (alk. paper)
        1. Food industry and trade—United States—Management. 2. Food service—United States—Management. 3. Food trucks—United States. 4. New business enterprises—United States. I. Mintzer, Richard. II. Entrepreneur Press.
    HD9005.S73 2015
    647.95—dc23   2015003797

Printed in the United States of America

20 19 18 17 16   10 9 8 7 6 5 4 3 2 1

Contents

Chapter 2

Planning a Business

Chapter 3

What's On the Menu?

▲

Chapter 7

If You Park It, They Will Come—or Not: Marketing, Promotion, and Pricing 89

Chapter 8

Mobile Event Catering 103

Chapter 9

The All-Important Costs 113

Chapter 10

Finding Funding 125

Chapter 11

Franchising 135

▲

Contents

Acknowledgments

'd like to thank Jere Calmes for the opportunity to write this book and Jillian McTigue for the opportunity to update it. It was great fun to write largely because of the input from so many helpful individuals who take great pride in their work.

I'd also like to thank Eric Weiner from FoodTrucksin. com, Zach Brooks, founder and owner, Midtownlunch. com; Van Leeuwen Artisan Ice Cream; Cody and Kristen Fields, Mmmpanadas, Austin, TX; Michelle Lozuaway and Josh Lanahan, Fresh Local, Portsmouth, NH; Scott Baitinger and Steve Mai, Streetza, Milwaukee; Adria Shimada, Parfait

Ice Cream, Seattle; Celine Legros of Les Caneies de Celine, New York (also thanks for the great sample pastries); Joe Rubin of FundingPost CT; Mike Boyd, Cart-King; Robert Smith, All Star Carts & Kiosks; Kris Ruby, The Ruby Media Group LLC, Westchester, NY; Eric Stite, founder and president, Franchise Business Review; Nancy Biberman, Marcus Gotay and Kerry McLean, of WHEDco where they walked me through their fabulous commercial kitchens in the Bronx. Thank you all very much.

Preface

If you enjoy cooking, or simply dining out, it is likely that you have dreamed of owning your own restaurant. Even non-entrepreneurial types have had the fantasy. I've always loved dining out and fantasized about a unique restaurant where people order ethnic foods in advance that are flown in from all over the world and prepared for special occasions. Obviously this would be quite an undertaking, and a very high-end dining experience. Because it's my fantasy restaurant, I need not worry about the particulars or the costs. If your fantasy involves serving lots of great food to hungry customers but without the high overhead of a restaurant lease, then a food cart, kiosk, trailer, truck, or bustaurant may be for you. These colorful vehicles with their great food, social contact, and audience looking for low-cost eats have made the mobile food industry the latest craze among a new generation of foodies.

The following chapters provide an overview of the mobile food industry and what it takes to start a business here. While the modes of transportation vary, the concept behind the idea of good food and "takin' it to the streets" remains. There is also information about being a business owner. If you embrace this new culture and don't mind the hard work, you could have a marvelous time earning a living as a mobile food entrepreneur.

From Hot Dog Wagons to Bustaurants

Today, a new generation of street food lovers are lining up at food trucks and food carts like never before. Little do they know that neither food trucks nor food carts are new to the streets of American cities. Like so many other popular trends, they are the latest version of a long-standing part of American and world culture. Yet the street food industry has never enjoyed so much publicity or notoriety. It is booming—to the delight of some foodies and the chagrin of others, especially those who own restaurants that are not witnessing the same long lines as their mobile counterparts.

But before taking a look at this burgeoning industry and giving you the lowdown on how to get started, here's a brief lesson in mobile food history. After all, even the modern carmaker knows a little bit about Henry Ford and the growth of the auto industry.

The History of Mobile Food

The concept of mobile food actually began centuries ago when carts brought food to armies at war in Europe and other parts of the world. Farmers also used carts to bring their foods to nearby towns, often stopping to sell goods along the way. In the United States in cities such as New York, immigrants who landed at Ellis Island took jobs selling food from carts. In fact, street food vendors as far back as the 17th century helped New York City's rapid growth, because foods were readily available to merchants, business owners, and inhabitants of the growing city. These foods were mostly taken home to be cooked, rather than eaten straight from the cart. However, not unlike the growing battles between restaurant owners and food truck owners today, public market owners and street food vendors had their share of disputes. In 1691, an ordinance was passed that said food vendors could not open until two hours after the public markets were open.

While carts were around for years, the forerunner of the food truck in the United States was the chuckwagon, which carried food and cooking equipment for the wagon trains as they headed west. In 1866, Charles Goodnight, a Texas rancher, gathered foods in a wagon to accompany long cattle drives. The chuckwagons were especially strong so they could carry a Dutch oven, a cast iron pot with legs, plus a cook's worktable, utensils, and the food, which was known as chuck. Hence the term "chuckwagon." Stew, roast beef, grits, boiled potatoes, beans, and fruit pies were typically on the chuckwagon menus.

Shortly thereafter, in 1872, the first diner was established. It was in a trailer. Diners—complete with service counters dominating the interior, a food preparation area against the back wall, and floor-mounted stools for the customers—were a means of bringing restaurants to new locations in the 1920s and '30s. Many were modeled after railroad dining cars. Some took on the art deco design of the time, and most were pulled on flat back trucks.

The next significant mobile food vehicles were World War I mobile canteens, also known as field kitchens. Often field kitchens were made up of two pieces: the supply section and the rear oven area. These original trailers, typically pulled by horses, evolved into mobile canteen trucks of World War II, providing food and drinks for soldiers as they returned from overseas. When the war ended, the idea of mobile food continued. The proliferation of highways led to the growing suburbs, and as a result, offices and factories also began to spread out, moving away from the big cities. As a result, early snack trucks became common at factories and construction sites.

It was also in the postwar years of the early 1950s that ice cream trucks began cruising the suburbs, to the delight of children in both the United States and Canada. On the early ice cream trucks, the driver would turn a crank to sound the chimes and let it be known that the ice cream truck was on the way. The ice cream was kept cold by blocks of dry ice. Of course by the 1950s, food carts had already become a staple at amusement parks and other venues where people gathered for fun. In fact, it was in 1936 that Oscar Mayer rolled out the first portable hot dog cart and called it the Wiener mobile. It was a big hit.

From the 1960s and '70s on, sandwich trucks and lunch wagons, as they were called, became a staple in all parts of America. Meanwhile, urban areas, tight for space, were able to squeeze in numerous hot dog, ice cream, soda, and pretzel carts wherever foot traffic was heavy. By the late 20th century, there was enough modern technology available to make it more feasible to keep a wider range of foods fresh cooked and served from a mobile vehicle. As a result, today's food truck owner and mobile caterer have more options than ever before.

The Industry Is Booming

There is still no official count of food trucks in the United States, with estimates ranging from 20,000 to 3 million, depending on which statistics you find. The actual number probably falls in the 30,000 to 50,000 range. The problem is that no national records are kept in conjunction with the local licensing. In addition, there are a growing number of food carts as well as kiosks which are a fixture in malls as well as at train and bus stations, airports, stadiums, conference centers, resorts, and other locations in recent years.

Food industry observers claim that the food truck business is increasing in recent years largely in response to the slow-growing economy. People are seeking inexpensive breakfasts and/or lunches. Also, employees today are often pressed for time, with more work and shorter lunch hours. These factors make the mobile food concept more appealing than ever.

From an entrepreneurial standpoint, kiosks, carts, trailers, and food trucks have a lower overhead than restaurants and can be moved if one location does not

tip

While the mobility of a cart, trailer, or truck sounds appealing and even liberating as one drives from place to place, most successful mobile food vehicles find they spend the vast majority of time in a few regular locations.

generate enough business. Rather than having to determine where to open a restaurant and worry about the old real estate adage "location, location, location," the owner can actually drive to a new location, location, location if business is doing poorly.

The Benefits of Mobile Food

Because food is a necessity and you add the convenience of having food favorites right outside a particular location—or inside with a kiosk—you meet several needs by serving mobile food. First, you offer food that is cost friendly because you need not pay wait people or busboys. You also offer the convenience of quick service. In many cases you provide food choices that can save those on a busy schedule from the need to sit down. Typically they can eat street foods while en route to their next destination. Finally, mobile food is often fun to eat and (if it's good) great to talk about.

The Increase in Mobile Food Businesses

In a slow economy, many people want to try other skills that they were not using at those desk jobs from which they were let go. For others, it's a chance to take on a second way of making money. Then there are restaurant owners who want to make up for falling profits, while also using mobile vehicles to market their brick-and-mortar businesses.

The boom is partly the result of new technology that allows for safer, cost-effective food preparation inside a mobile vehicle. From freezers to ovens to grills, the latest innovations offer more possibilities. Additionally, cleaning products have made it easier to keep a vehicle sanitary and up to code—a long-time concern and major criticism of food trucks.

There are also well-known food companies—from food chains like Johnny Rockets, Sizzler, or White Castle to food manufacturers such as Taste D-Lite or Colorado's organic burrito makers, EVOL, that were brave pioneers when they took trucks to the streets to increase sales and/or market their brands to new customers.

Yes, there are many reasons why the mobile truck industry is going bananas, so to speak. Although there aren't many banana-themed food trucks . . . yet.

tip

It's important to serve ready-to-eat foods. More than 91 percent of revenue for street vendors comes from the sale of take-away food and drink for immediate consumption rather than for later consumption at another location, according to IBIS World a national publisher of industry research reports.

Can Food Trucks Be Profitable?

The National Restaurant Association estimates that food trucks generate $650 million in annual revenue, roughly 1 percent of U.S. restaurant sales. Intuit expects that market share to jump to 3 or 4 percent in the next five years.

Among the reasons why food trucks can be profitable is that they can hit a slightly higher price point than their fast food counterparts. In addition they have lower startup costs than restaurants, coming in between $55,000 to $75,000, compared to $250,000 to $500,000 for a restaurant. As for profits, in a 2013 review of food truck economics from Priceonomics, it was estimated that a successful food truck could bring in $500,000-plus per year, with one food truck owner quoting $200,000 as the break-even point.

Mathematically, it is estimated that if a three-hour lunch or dinner window can bring in $1,000 over five lunches/dinners per week that would be $5,000 per week or $250,000 per year. Trucks bringing in $2,000 per day could top that $500,000 total. Of course, this does not factor in special events that may bring in more per day and inclement weather that might shut down food trucks for days or weeks at a time.

The answer to the question about profitability, however, is "yes" and as food truck owners learn the tricks of the trade to minimize expenses and maximize potential revenues through prime locations, marketing efforts, and most effective pricing, they can enjoy profits for the fruits of their labor.

Goin' Mobile: Your Options

Even before you decide what foods to sell, you'll want to consider how you want to sell them. We will talk later in greater detail about these mobile possibilities, but for now it's a good idea to familiarize yourself with the most popular options, which include food kiosks, carts, trucks, and buses. Yes, you could probably use a motorcycle or bicycle to your advantage, but we'll leave those to your creative ability.

Clearly, your decision on how to sell your foods will depend on:

- Your startup money, budget, and potential for returns
- Your commitment to the business: part time, full time, etc.
- Your creative ideas and what it will take to fulfill them
- Your experience at running a business

▲

- The size of the business you want to start
- Your ideal demographic (Obviously if you plan to work inside of local shopping malls, a kiosk is a better plan than a food truck.)

These are a few of the considerations you will look at as you proceed, but for now, let's introduce the common mobile food entities.

Food Kiosks

While the word kiosk is still fairly new to most Westerners, it actually dates back to the 13th century when they were set up in places such as India, Persia, and Pakistan to sell goods.

In modern times, electronic information kiosks have become popular as a means of pushing buttons to gather data. However, food kiosks, not unlike those used seven centuries ago, are essentially booths or food stands that are temporary or mobile facilities used to prepare and sell food. Malls and stadiums are popular locations for food kiosks, which sell anything from pretzels to ice cream to hot dogs to more elaborate fare.

Although kiosks may have wheels, they are not mobile under their own power and in most cases need to be assembled. Most kiosks are rectangular and have room for two people to work within or stand behind, preparing and serving the food. They also have counter space and overhead signage.

The low overhead, flexibility, and ease by which a kiosk can be opened and closed are among the reasons why they're so popular. They are also an excellent choice in areas where your outdoor selling season would be limited by cold or nasty weather. Of course, the size of the kiosk limits the inventory, so it's important for a kiosk owner to carry as much as possible and price accordingly so that she can make money off of what is on hand each day. Because they are usually operating indoors, kiosk owners typically sign licensing agreements at malls, stadiums, movie theaters, or other locations. Many major food businesses such as Ben & Jerry's and Baskin-Robbins franchise express kiosks.

Food Carts and Concession Trailers

The food cart and the concession trailer have been around for decades and combined are a multibillion-dollar industry today. The best known have always been hot dog and ice cream carts. They are among the most cost-effective ways to start a mobile food business because the carts are typically pulled by your car, truck, van, or pushed by hand. Food is either prepared in advance, purchased ready to sell—like ice cream pops or cups of Italian ices—then stored, and either heated up or pulled from the freezer. Carts are also fairly easy to maintain and in many counties and communities require less licensing than the full-sized food trucks. It is also cost effective if you choose to own several carts and hire friends, family, or outside employees to help run them for you.

Unlike kiosks, which are typically found indoors (although they can be outdoors), food carts are typically outdoor businesses. An advantage of a food cart is easy mobility. Because food carts do not take up much room, it is easy to change locations.

There are two basic types of food carts. One has room for the vendor to sit or stand inside and serve food through a window. The other utilizes all the space in the cart for food storage and cooking equipment, which is typically a grill. The precise type of cart is determined largely by the food being offered. Espresso and coffee carts, for example, are made specifically with hot beverages in mind.

Modern day food cart owners have cleaned up the somewhat greasy reputation of street food vendors. They have also expanded their menus. Kebobs and gyros came on the cart scene awhile ago, and vegetarian and Mediterranean salads have also caught on, as well as fish and chips. Some are offering interesting breakfast choices, such as the Asada Food Cart in Denver, which is getting rave reviews for their breakfast burrito with steak, eggs, green chili, and potatoes. Trailers, like carts, do not move under their own power, limiting their potential locations. Food trailers are often found at fairs, carnivals, sporting events, or other places where they can be unhitched and sit for awhile. Unlike most carts, trailers allow for cooking and have room for two or three people inside. Skillet Street Food in Seattle operates from an Airstream trailer with a full kitchen within. In short, a trailer can provide more options than a cart but is still less expensive than a truck.

Food Trucks

The food truck can carry any number of foods, and in some cases more sophisticated equipment for storing, serving, cooking, and preparing foods. Of course how much actual cooking you can do onboard the truck will vary from city to city or county to county.

The traditional food trucks were known for providing lunches, typically stocking sandwiches, kebobs, tacos, burgers, and other standard fare for the lunch crowd. Many have expanded to include healthier vegetarian and vegan offerings, as well as the not-so-healthy barbecue ribs. They do big business in corporate parks and places that have limited access to restaurants. Most food trucks are stocked from concessionaires, but there is a growing

tip

It is recommended that you start with a few items that you know how to prepare well and expand as you grow. Carts and kiosks typically sell a couple of items. Food truck owners should follow suit. It makes starting and running your business much easier.

number that are associated with fast food and mid-level restaurants. Sizzler and California Pizza Kitchen, for example, are putting together their own food trucks as are other chains.

Larger than carts, trucks can carry more food and handle more business. However, food trucks need more space to park both when doing business and when "off-duty."

Essentially, there are two types of food trucks. One is the mobile food preparation vehicle (MFPV) where food is prepared as customers wait, hopefully not very long. The other is the industrial catering vehicle (ICV), which sells only prepackaged foods. An MFPV costs more than an ICV, and both cost more than a food cart. For example, a used hotdog cart may cost under $2,500, while a retrofitted used food truck would typically cost $40,000 or more. A newly designed food truck retrofitted MFPV with new all equipment could cost you upwards of $100,000.

Complying with additional health department rules and regulations can also drive up food truck costs. Clearly, a smaller truck, a used truck, and/or a truck with limited equipment costs less. Therefore, it is up to you to determine whether you'll be cooking in the truck, preparing food off-site and serving from the vehicle, or selling prepared and prepackaged foods.

The Border Grill Truck serves up gourmet tacos, quesadillas, ceviches, and other Mexican favorites in and around the Los Angeles area.

Gourmet Food Trucks

Basically the same as a food truck, the gourmet food truck takes food quality to a higher level. Of the numerous food trucks licensed to do business in the Los Angeles area, only about 200 are considered "gourmet." They are run by ambitious young chefs who offer cuisine not typically found in food trucks, such as Rajas fries topped with fire-roasted poblano chiles, caramelized onions, and shawarma-marinated steak with Jack cheese found at Frysmith in Los Angeles. Many gourmet trucks have specialties and themes. In addition, they let their clientele know where they'll be parked through their websites and social media sites such as Twitter as well as through mobile apps. While food trucks need not have kitchens, gourmet trucks are more likely to have food prepared on the spot—and high-end food at that.

At the start of the new gourmet food truck craze, Los Angeles was clearly the place to find such high-end dining. Now, however, New York had gained its share of such fancy food vehicles, such as the Rickshaw Dumpling Bar and The Dessert Truck, founded by a former Le Cirque pastry chef. And as the concept of serving fine food rolls along, other cities from Portland, Oregon, to St Louis and on down to Miami's South Beach are jumping on the foodie bandwagon with their own regional favorites. Food Network chef Ingrid Hoffmann's black and pink Latin Burger and Taco Truck, for example, has become quite the rage in Miami.

The Mobile Catering Business

Mobile catering trucks can be defined in a variety of ways and can overlap with mobile food trucks. For my purposes here, I'll highlight three differences. First, a catering truck is hired for a specific event such as a picnic, party, or fair. Secondly,

---

Price Value

According to a survey by Emergent Research of customers in San Francisco, one of the hot spots for food trucks, more than 90 percent of lunchtime customers surveyed rated food truck quality as either excellent (43 percent) or good (48 percent). About 50 percent characterized dinner cuisine as excellent.

The survey also found that most patrons felt they were getting good, not great value. The average customer spent $9.80 for lunch and $14.99 for dinner (per person). And while only a few (8 percent) spend less than $8 (per person), nearly half (45 percent) spent less than $10.

▲

the person hiring the catering vehicle can select from a catering menu. Third, a catering vehicle can be used to transport the foods, which are then handed out from inside the truck or set up at the event or gathering, typically on trays or buffet style.

This can mean providing the food to be served outdoors or parking and serving from the truck as the food trucks do. The differences are primarily in the manner of doing business. Nonetheless, the need for a reliable vehicle, licensing, permits, sanitary conditions, a business plan, and startup money are quite similar to the requirements of a mobile food business.

One of the advantages of a mobile catering business is that you are not risking as much in inventory because you are cooking and bringing food as ordered for the upcoming party or special event. Therefore, you are covered for your food costs. You also have a specific destination, so you need not worry whether or not your favorite destinations will be busy or not. Typically, you are less dependent on good weather because many catered functions will be indoors. As long as you can get there with the food, you are usually OK. Of course, you do need to line up enough work to support your business. The difference between a mobile catering business and other catering businesses is that you are using the mobility of the truck to show up rather than having a catering hall or venue.

The mobile catering business affords you flexibility as to when you take jobs and where. Still, the more available you are, the better off you will be.

> ### tip ⓘ
> Have you heard of the 80–20 rule in sales? This is a long-standing business principle that says that 80 percent of your business will come from repeat customers and 20 percent from new customers. For caterers or mobile food vendors, this means, as the Simon and Garfunkel song says, "Keep the Customer Satisfied."

Bustaurants

As the name implies, a bustaurant is not a truck but a bus, often a double-decker with the lower level for the kitchen and the upper level for customers to sit and eat. They are new. Some boast gourmet foods, while others have more standard fare. The idea is to provide seating and be a restaurant on wheels. The idea started primarily in San Francisco and Los Angeles, with Londoners also watching some of their famed double decker buses transformed into restaurants on wheels. Now, you'll find bustaurants in various towns and cities around the country such as the Food Fighters bustaurant in Hartsville, Alabama servin' rockin' tacos out of an old school bus. Needless to say, they require more room to park and additional licensing in most counties, and are more costly to start because the buses need to be fully refurbished to include grills, refrigerators, vents, and so on. Many food trucks, on the other hand, are designed and built with both cooking and serving food in mind.

Some bustaurants, take diners on a private mobile eating adventure. Others park and serve customers as they board at a specific location. Some of the buses cook the food while parked—it all depends on what is or is not legal in your jurisdiction. Because they are very new, more and more innovative bustaurants will literally be rolling out as you read this book. Yet because they are so new, the jury is still out on whether they are a passing fad (pun intended) or they will catch on. Much of what is discussed here as necessary for food trucks is also necessary for bustaurants, including marketing, costs, permits, menus, etc.

Your Customers

It is estimated, not surprisingly, that the largest demographic group for the food truck industry are the 18 to 34 year olds, with strong numbers from college campuses and 9 to 5ers. However, as the Baby Boomer generation (50+) now tops 76 million people, that is also becoming a growing demographical for seniors on a budget and those looking to try something new . . . or old, depending on whether they enjoyed the hot dog carts of previous generations.

There are several demographic groups that can provide potential customers. Who you focus on influences your menu, locations, and daily schedule of food preparation.

The Breakfast Club

First you want to be ready for the morning crowd. Coffee is your number-one priority, so make sure you are making it fresh and good. Your customers want a good cup of coffee on their way to work, with maybe a Danish, bagel, or croissant. You'll get some juice lovers, so be prepared. Fruit is also a new, healthy, morning favorite. If you're parked by office parks or on streets lined with office buildings, expect a lot of people on their way into the office. This breakfast club does not usually stop for an elaborate breakfast, so keep it simple. Be ready with easy-to-serve foods, and give them their shot of caffeine with a friendly smile to start their day. More than any other group, these customers operate from force of habit. If they like your food, coffee, prices, and quickness, they'll come back again and again without even thinking about it.

The Lunch Bunch

This is the bread-and-butter group for many truck and cart owners, no pun intended (well, maybe). Here you can be more diverse in your offerings because the lunch crowd has more time to decide what they want than the breakfast club, whose members are often on the run.

▲

However, whether you are parked by a construction site or the corporate offices of a Fortune 500 company, there is still a time element to contend with. You need to be able to serve and move on to the next customer quickly. Typically, if someone has 45 minutes to an hour for lunch (and in today's overworked corporate culture, many people have just 15 minutes to grab the food to eat at their desks), you want to minimize the lines by being ready to take orders and serve. After all, if customers have time to wait around, they can sit in a restaurant.

Your other advantage is prices below those in restaurants, so keep them down. Zach Brooks of midtownlunch.com says $10 is the typical cutoff point for most street foods.

Much of today's lunch bunch is also looking for creative and healthy choices, although many will still go with the standard hot dog or taco and soda. If you can, mix it up a little between standard fare and your creative ideas. Lunchers usually travel in pairs (or more), and they may not all have the sophisticated tastes. Ethnic cuisine is a favorite, but again, consider milder and more mainstream options for a wider lunch crowd. Keep the menu manageable because the more you offer, the more you need to have in stock—and space is limited.

Tastes for Tourists and Attendees

Tourists, business travelers, and attendees at conferences and special events are around for a reason. Know your customers. The crowd at a NASCAR event probably

---

No Training Necessary

Cody Fields was a mechanical engineer building water treatment plants in South America. He spent five years working, traveling, and eating a lot of empanadas. Finally, the Texas native returned home, settled in Austin, and went back to school. He wanted to do something different but didn't know quite what that new career was going to be. While in school, he met Kristen, who would eventually become his wife. Both Cody and Kristen enjoyed cooking, but neither had any formal training. Cody took a job in a bank and knew it wasn't for him. "The first day at the bank I was seated in a cubical. I immediately knew from day one that I needed to get out of there," says Cody. So, one night in 2007, while attending the opening of a new neighborhood bar, Cody and Kristen cooked six-dozen gourmet empanadas as a grand opening gift to welcome the new bar owners. "They loved the empanadas," recalls Cody, and the bar owner immediately asked how they could get more. "Give me two weeks and I'll get back to you," replied an ambitious Cody. In those two weeks, he rented a commercial kitchen,

---

No Training Necessary, continued

got his food-manufacturing license, and secured all the necessary permits to start cooking.

Together Cody and Kristen brainstormed ideas for recipes and fillings and after two weeks they were ready to start selling empanadas. Over the next three months the cooking couple picked up a few more clients. The food truck craze had yet to begin in Austin. "There was a cupcake truck and a crepe truck, plus some of the old taco trucks that went to construction sites," he explains.

Cody bought an old pizza truck on eBay for about $20,000 and a generator for another $10,000. He fixed up the truck and got the necessary licenses. He also painted the truck bright red. The truck stood out, and Mmmpanadas was officially on the road. Over the years the Austin Mmmpanadas truck has been written up in *GQ* and twice in *Southern Living*. Cody has long since left that bank job, and the empanadas that he and Kristen continue to make are now sold not only from the truck but also in stores all over Austin, including Whole Foods. They are still looking to expand their retail business. And it all started by cooking 72 gourmet empanadas (mmmpanadas.com).

The bright red Mmmpanadas truck services the night crowd in Austin, Texas.

has different tastes than the attendees at an environmental convention. Stock up accordingly. Tourists are often anxious to taste something that epitomizes your city. If you're at a tourist location, such as Central Park in Manhattan or Coney Island, a New York City hot dog would be a tourist-style treat, as would jambalaya on Bourbon Street in New Orleans.

If you are centered around a theme, such as cupcakes, you'll need to plan your locations accordingly. Of course, products like cupcakes have a wide appeal, so unless other dessert trucks are in an area, you can always find your way into the mix.

The Late Nighters

When the clubs or nighttime sporting events let out, people are hungry. Knowing where to find the late night crowd means knowing the nightlife in your city and being prepared to satisfy their appetites for food or munchies, as the case may be. Typically this crowd is looking for simple snacks. Those who are inebriated and cannot pronounce elaborate dishes, don't usually want them at 2 A.M. Coffee is always a mainstay as are snack foods and hand-held favorites like pizza and tacos.

Planning a Business

A s exciting as it may seem to jump into a new business, it doesn't happen without significant planning, at least if you want to have a good chance of success. To start, you need to have the right mind-set and the skills to go into the business of your dreams. You also need to understand what it takes to be an entrepreneur. It usually starts with a great idea or an opportunity that presents itself, such as buying into an existing business or a franchise.

In this chapter we take a look at the first part of the business equation—you, the business owner. Then we look at some of the planning that you will want to do before venturing out into the field, or in this case, hitting the streets.

Are You Hungry?

Starting a business means being your own boss. It also means getting ready to roll up your sleeves and get greasy if necessary. The mobile food business is going strong. You'll want to act fast, before too many players get into the game. There is only so much room on the streets. In fact, many city governments are aware that a limit on licenses may be necessary, if it's not already on the books (such as in New York City). Nonetheless, you cannot take too many shortcuts. Learning about the business inside and out is key to starting any venture.

To earn money in mobile food service means being hungry. It means having menu items your competitors don't have (or at least making your own unique versions of popular favorites) and finding locations that aren't already teeming with competitors. Mobile lunch trucks have long been based upon the simple concept of bringing quality food to people in areas where there are not many other food choices. Now it is also about bringing cost-friendly options to places where there are other food choices. Faster service and lower prices allow you to compete with brick-and-mortar eateries. However, to succeed you need to serve good food and maintain the highest levels of cleanliness.

Not only a can-do attitude, but also an eye for detail is important because there are numerous details involved. You also need to be organized, able to set up and follow a working routine, and be ready to make changes if your routine isn't working. You don't need to be a chef, but knowing how to cook is a big plus. You can, however, simply know quality food, and/or have great marketing abilities. And finally you also need a little bit of daring because running a food truck isn't a standard office job or restaurant position. It means

warning

While food carts and trucks are competitive among themselves, they do share one commonality. Neither is particularly well liked by many brick-and-mortar business owners, especially restaurateurs and food shop owners. Reports of such business owners calling the cops on food trucks abound. Other incidents from slashed tires to harassed customers have also been reported. Because you are the newcomer, you need to be aware and respectful of existing business owners and do your best to avoid ruffling their feathers.

running a mobile enterprise where you may be in several locations each week, some for better and some for worse.

Do You Have the Drive?

While it may look easy, the food truck industry takes a lot of hard work. For Scott Baitinger and partner Steve Mai, who run the famous Streetza pizza truck in Milwaukee, Wisconsin, a typical day starts three or four hours before taking the truck out on the road. "First we'll stop at Sam's Club or Restaurant Depot and pick up fresh ingredients. Then we go to our off-site commissary kitchen where we do all the prep work, which includes rolling the dough, making sauces, cutting the vegetables, and all of the things you really can't do in a 10-by-10 truck," explains Baitinger, who still works a day job as a marketing manager for a major mattress company while handling the truck on nights and weekends. Mai runs the weekday shifts except at times in the winter when nobody in Milwaukee wants to trek outside in three feet of snow—not even for pizza.

Then the Streetza team, which also includes a small staff on various shifts, park at well-selected locations and prepare and sell foods. "We put on the toppings and assemble and bake the food in the truck, but because of the size of pizzas, it's not the kind of thing you can make on the truck." Some vendors sell food that can be cooked on their trucks, notes Baitinger. Some cities allow cooking on a vehicle, while others require a separate, off-site commercial kitchen be used. This requirement differs from city to city.

At the end of a day, which is typically when they run out of food or the crowds have dissipated, comes the cleanup. "It's a lot like a restaurant cleanup with stainless steel cleaners, scrubbing, mopping, and making sure everything is in perfect shape to start again tomorrow," adds Baitinger.

Most mobile food business owners follow a similar set routine, whether it includes running the kiosk, cart, or truck themselves or having employees run it. The routine may include very early morning food shopping a few days a week, if not everyday. Then there is stocking the kiosk or vehicle and heading to your destination(s). There is also a need to take some time during the day for marketing, usually via Twitter or another social media. Most mobile food vendors

tip

By hand or on your computer, map out your day. Having your schedule on paper allows you to look closely and possibly find ways to improve it. A printed version also lets you hire employees and plug them into the routine more easily. Most importantly, your daily or weekly schedule helps you not forget to do something.

▲

work roughly ten hours a day. There are also days in which a business owner needs to sit down in a quiet office space, preferably at home with his feet up, and do all of the bookkeeping: paying taxes and bills, renewing licenses, and handling other fun paperwork responsibilities.

The work is tiring and the day is long. Can you handle such a day on a regular basis?

Do You Have the Skills?

What skills do you need to run a mobile food business? Some degree of experience owning, running, or working in a restaurant environment can be helpful. However, while many food truck owners come from a food background, many others come from marketing, teaching, and other professions. Foodies and entrepreneurs come from many backgrounds, but they do need certain skills to excel in this business.

Marketing

"One of the most important skills is marketing," explains Baitinger, adding that about 25 percent of the people who start food trucks come from the marketing end and hire chefs and people who know about the food industry. "It's a very important part of the equation. You need to have a menu targeted to potential customers, and today you need to know how to use social media tools that are out there to your advantage," adds Baitinger. For Cody Fields it was a matter of having a bright red truck for his empanadas in a town that, at that time, only had boring white food trucks. "We stood out and generated a lot of attention," says Fields of the Mmmpanadas truck he and his wife have run for the past six years.

Customer Service

There are constant interactions with customers, whether you are waiting on them or have staffers to heat up and serve them food. Either way, such customer interaction is a key aspect of your business. Interaction includes knowing how to engage customers, have patience with them, answer their questions, and always provide polite service.

Multitasking

You need to be good at multitasking to run a mobile food business. Preparing and/ or heating food, taking orders, collecting money, and giving correct change while also cleaning up spills or other minor hazards at the same time may be required. Even if you are not in the truck but in your off-site kitchen, you'll need to cook and prepare various foods at once, manage your kitchen help, handle your marketing, and stay on top of the clean-up process that is such a vital part of the business.

Food Knowledge

You don't have to be an expert chef to know what tastes good and what you believe others will like. You do have to understand food, good quality, good prices in your part of the country, good food combinations, and how foods complement one another. You also need to become very astute at knowing how foods are best prepared, and the best ways to serve them and keep them fresh. From cookbooks to the Food Channel to websites galore, there are many ways to enhance your food knowledge and find recipes and cooking tips.

The Ability to Try New Things (and Be Creative)

"We experimented for six months with various pizza topping," says Scott Baitinger. In time, he and his partner created a menu based on what they found tasty and original. They also got creative. One of the most popular Streetza pizzas featured fresh blue corn, a mix of cheeses, and a king crab leg on every slice. Of course, when you have some hits like the crab leg pizza, you will inevitably also have some misses. "We tried pickled herring pizza—not very good at all," says Baitinger of one of their many culinary experiments that never reached the customers. In any competitive business, it's important to be ready to think out of the box to create new innovative products to sell.

Repair Skills

When you're driving a truck around, no matter how well you think everything is tied or bolted down, there will still be things that go wrong. "In any kitchen there will be things that break down," says Cody Fields, adding that it helps if you are good at repairing things. Of course, there are also repairs needed on the vehicle. Food truck owners generally agree that while being out and about, you need to be somewhat resilient and ready to deal with any number of daily challenges—from a broken generator to a fryer that isn't frying to a flat tire. There is no maintenance staff or IT specialist to call, so you're on your own. Being handy is a big plus. "Kitchens have their own issues and trucks can also have a host of issues. When you put those two together, you can get some exciting times," says Cody.

New Media Skills

One of the reasons that food trucks have become so popular is that they are using new media to their advantage. From Twitter to smartphone applications, truck owners are in regular communication with their customers, letting them know where they will be and when. Learning how to tweet and use the other popular social media tools is very important for marketing and building up your brand in this new street food culture. In many cases, mobile communication builds a loyal following. Streetza is among the vast majority of food trucks that interact regularly with its loyal following via Twitter. This helps you find great locations and receive suggestions for menu items. The fans even named the Streetza truck. Twitter, social media sites, and apps, helps food trucks draw a crowd much like the jingle of the Mister Softee truck brought kids running for ice cream.

Stamina

It may not be a skill, but being in shape helps in the mobile food business. Consider the lifting, standing, and movement involved in a typical day. Adria Shimada who owns the Parfait Ice Cream truck and recently opened her own Parfait ice cream shop, both in Seattle, noted that when she started out in the business she didn't realize how exhausting it could be. "You've got to be in fairly good shape," says Adria, who, with help, loads vats of ice cream in and out of freezers, and serves fans ice cream for hours.

Number Skills

You need not be a math major, but having a good head for number is a big plus. From recipes and measurements in the kitchen to bookkeeping, pricing, calculating profit margins, and keeping an eye on your budget, you will use plenty of numbers every day. Your calculator can help, but you need to be able to make determinations about whether the numbers it gives you look good or not.

Can You Compete?

Because the mobile food business is growing quickly, you need to have a competitive nature to succeed, especially in Los Angeles where food trucks are lining the streets. You need a keen eye for finding a competitive edge, that special something that sets you apart from the other trucks, trailers, buses, carts, or kiosks. The same goes for mobile catering businesses.

While competition is discussed in greater detail in the marketing section, it is important that you go into business with the idea that you are not just another fish in a giant pond, or you will get swallowed up. To be competitive:

- You need to approach the business with an eye for what your competitors are doing.
- You need to see which food trucks are generating the longest lines and why.
- You need to know your competitors' prices.
- You need to find out which mobile catering company is at the top of people's lists and figure out what it offers.
- You need to approach business with the keen eye of a detective, looking for clues that tell you why one company is succeeding and another is not.

Part of your pre business acumen should be due diligence. If you don't do your homework, you will likely fail in a competitive business. Market research is one of the first steps in starting any business. Scoping out the competition in this case is imperative because the competition may be five miles away one day and parked right across the street the next.

tip

Get into social media, and read what the foodies are saying about their favorite mobile food vendors and local restaurants. Get a feel for their favorite ideas from food to promotional items. Find out what the culture is all about, read reviews of food trucks on Yelp, visit some of the popular food truck locations. Besides tasting the food of your competitors, you'll want to get a feel for the buzz. Talk to customers, and when you're on your own jot down notes on what you have learned.

Business Goals

Mobile food success falls into several categories depending largely on what the owners are seeking from the business. Your goals will be based on your own situation, including your lifestyle, desired income, and other business endeavors.

Starting a business means you have the opportunity to take a new direction, or even many directions since you are mobile. Running a business provides an opportunity to follow your own dreams. It allows you to express yourself as well as make a living on your own schedule. Yes, you will need persistence and hard work to make a go of a new business. Yes, there will be times you question whether or not it will be worth it. And yes, there will be times when you may need to shift gears and make some major changes. A positive aspect is that as a business owner you are in control and everything comes back to you. Of course the negative aspect is that as a business owner you are in control and everything comes back to you. Clearly, there are two sides to taking on such responsibility. You get the glory and to enjoy the profits when all goes well. You get blame and have to deal with the losses when all goes poorly.

So, why start a business?

- To be in charge
- To have greater flexibility
- For personal expression
- To utilize specific skills (often those not used when working for someone else)
- To better control your own destiny
- To have an opportunity to do better financially
- To be socially and environmentally responsible
- To interact with your community
- To create jobs for other people
- To work with family, friends, and people you actually like

These are among the reasons to start any new business. Hopefully some are among your reasons for starting a mobile food business.

Part-Time Business

For some people, running a mobile food business on the weekends and/ or at night can provide an extra source of income. However, as Cody Fields of Mmmpanadas found out after a year of having a desk job by day and driving the food truck by night, it can become quite exhausting. In addition, the cost of buying and maintaining a full-sized truck may not be offset by part-time usage. Some truck owners keep their full-time day jobs while having a partner who and staff running the truck on a full-time schedule. Other owners have enough money to hire people to run the truck while others use business partners, taking a behind-the-scenes role. Most food truck owners dive into the commitment head first and make it their number-one priority.

As for kiosk and food cart owners, some find that working weekends at special events can supplement a full-time income. It's still a lot of work, but overhead is lower than with a truck and there are profits to be made if the location is good.

Weekend mobile caterers have found that running their business on the side can be productive only if they take on what they can handle and have an inexpensive vehicle for transport. Remember, the more money you put into the vehicle, the more you need to recoup. If you keep expenses low, you can make money on a part-time basis with good marketing, a good product, and a schedule that is manageable. But don't book more than you can handle.

Full-Time Business

Full time means making the "big" commitment. You need enough volume to make this work and that comes from:

- Scouting the competition
- Learning the business
- Making sure you adhere to every city, town, and local ordinance
- Having all necessary permits and licenses and updating them regularly

tip

Set a weekly time to handle bookkeeping, paying taxes, paying bills, etc. It's very easy in your busy schedule to forget about these simple, yet vital, business requirements. Select a time and a place and enter it on your online calendar, Google Calendar app, smartphone, wall calendar, or any place else that helps you remember to take care of these business needs regularly.

Food Trucks Converge

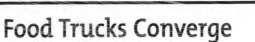

If you want to get the lowdown on a business, any business, attend their major events. In this case, the premier industry event is the annual Roam Mobile Food Conference, a must for staying on top of everything from food trucks to carts, to kiosks, and beyond. Started in 2013, this is an ideal event to attend if you are planning to join the mobile food industry.

Roam includes established business owners, up and coming entrepreneurs, food educators, suppliers, media, and government policy makers for a day and a half of learning, networking and fun. It's a place to learn about best practices, new trends, and technology and network with so many people from all aspects of the mobile food industry.

Roam is the first North American-wide industry conference serving the specific needs of mobile vendors. For more information go to roamconference.com or call 972-885-ROAM.

▲

- Having a good product that you've tested again and again
- Knowing your territory well
- Knowing your demographics
- Budgeting time and money wisely
- Setting up a daily and weekly routine and re-working it until it runs like clock-work
- Marketing, marketing, and marketing some more
- Rolling up your sleeves and working hard
- Hiring people you can count on and training them well
- Remembering to do your bookkeeping

Like most brick-and-mortar businesses, you need to have enough sales with a sufficient profit margin to make this endeavor worthwhile. Your advantages are that you will have a lower overhead than most brick-and-mortar businesses and you can change locations far more easily. Your disadvantages are that you can only charge so much for street food and your hours of operation are limited by various factors, including parking restrictions, the weather, and your inventory.

Extension of a Current Business

If you own a restaurant or if you are a food manufacturer, you may now be joining the many entrepreneurs taking their businesses to the streets. For many existing restaurant owners or food manufacturers the outside of the truck is a giant billboard. It helps spread the word about their food products and/or restaurant, while also bringing in some money and providing samples of what you make and/or sell. It is essentially a tasty way of getting your product in the mouths of more people.

Restaurant owners in several cities are giving out samples to draw customers to their establishments. The mobility allows them to reach different demographic audiences and, get their foods and their brand to places where the people are from sporting events to street fairs to local concerts and community gatherings.

Inroads to a Restaurant

Some food truck owners are restauranteur wannabes. Josh Lanahan and Michelle Lozuaway were owners of the popular Fresh Local truck in Portsmouth, New Hampshire. After a few excellent years with healthy food on wheels, they decided to open a restaurant called Street, serving the healthy items that were originally served from the truck, and more. They have since added a second eatery in Portsmouth called the Cemita Shack.

Erin and Dave Emmons, owners of the popular Lucky Taco food truck, in Manchester, Connecticut, moved from making food and serving it from their truck to cooking and serving from their new Lucky Taco Cantina on Main Street. Like their New England comrades in New Hampshire, they also opened a second restaurant just three weeks later called the Tap Room.

Another food truck transition, that is not all that uncommon, is using your wheels after hours to start a catering business. The Skillet Street Food truck in Seattle became so popular that it led to the Skillet Catering with 100 talented people running the show. Of course the gang at Skillet Street also runs the Skillet Diners.

Streetza has also made a triumphant transition into the catering world. "Roughly 75 percent of our sales now come from catering corporate events for clients ranging from car dealerships to Google," says Baitinger, who adds that being part of the food truck community is more important than fighting over issues like parking spots. "We call other truck owners that we are friendly with when we are asking to cater events and we are already booked," adds the Streetza co-founder.

Supported by an outstanding team of almost 100 talented people, Skillet Catering handles weddings, private parties, and corporate events throughout the Pacific Northwest. They also distribute their very own signature Bacon Jam product through retailers across the U.S. and Canada.

A growing number of food truck owners cater events on weekends or during the weeks in cold climates that they are otherwise shut down.

The Business Plan

Regardless of your entrepreneurial vision, a business plan is important in any endeavor, especially if you are hoping to attract some backers to help you foot the bill for that $100,000 specially refurbished truck you have your eye on. A well thought out business plan tells the story of your entrepreneurial dream and details your vision in a way that it can help you generate the necessary funding.

Even if you are not seeking backers, a business plan can help guide you through the process of gathering all the key information to keep you on track as you proceed.

There are books, articles, websites, and software packages designed to take you through the steps necessary to build a business plan. They usually come complete with templates to follow so you need not recreate the wheel. The inclusion of some business plan basics here is designed to get you to start thinking about possibilities, which you can fill in as you read through this book and decide on what kind of food(s) you'll be serving, the size of your vehicle, and your startup and operational costs.

A business plan is a way of organizing on paper all of the pieces of the puzzle, from your equipment needs to your various locations to ordering and shopping for food. Finally, it is a living, breathing document that can not only serve as a benchmark and also can be altered and expanded as your business grows and changes over the years.

Included in a typical business plan are the following:

1. *Executive summary.* This is a short, broad yet enticing summary of the business. What is the business all about, and why are you excited about it? Although it usually appears first, this section is often written last, after you have put all the pieces in place.

2. *Products and/or services.* Here you can include specific items that you will sell or services you will offer. Include foods and/or drinks that will be on your menu and other possibilities that you anticipate adding down the road. Explain their popularity and why they will be sought by your customers. Also explain what goes into making these culinary delights.

3. *Industry analysis.* Here you paint a picture of the mobile food industry in which your business will be a player. From your research, talk about the big picture and the growing popularity of mobile foods and/or catering. Back up your statements with facts and numbers. By researching and writing a few paragraphs on the mobile food business, you will also learn more about the industry.

4. *Competitive analysis.* This is huge! Do your research carefully and know whom you are up against. Be realistic. Listing the strengths and weaknesses of your direct competitors helps you determine where you will fit into the local market. Then see if you can provide something that your competitors do not offer. Do you have more menu options? Perhaps you have a combo with a drink that is cheaper than your competitor's prices. Maybe you've even created a new food combination like the Pirito, a flat rectangular cross between a panini and a burrito (golden crispy pita bread on outside and any number of foods inside) created a few years back by Josh Lanahan and Michelle Lozuaway when they owned the Fresh Local truck in Portsmouth, New Hampshire. Know your competition well and seek a competitive edge.

tip

Review your business plan first to make sure it tells the story of the business you envision. Next make sure it covers all of the key areas and leaves no stone unturned when it comes to running your business in a smooth manner. Finally, if you are planning to show your business plan to prospective backers, make sure to proofread it very carefully.

5. *Marketing and sales.* Once you have the details in place, you need to explain how you will let the world know you are in business. In this section, you discuss your plans for marketing and promoting your mobile food business as well as your plans for selling your products and services. Will you be setting up a website? Do you plan to use social media to get the word out about your business and your location? Are you planning to list your truck in directories and on websites and apps? Where will you be selling? Street locations? Festival and events? Do you do mobile theme catering? Parties? Outdoor events? Office parties?

   This is where to define your plan of attack. If you are seeking funding, this section is extremely important because backers want to know that you have thought about what you will be selling, to whom, and how you will reach your audience and build a following. Also include your pricing in conjunction with competitive pricing in your area.

6. *Management.* Another important section is management. Here you let readers know who is running the business. Potential financial backers are particularly interested in this information because they want to know to whom they are lending their money. Include all of the key people involved in making your business happen. If this is a solo venture, use a bio that features applicable experiences in your career or personal life that apply to this venture. It is very important that backers believe in you, so don't sell yourself short.

7. *Operations.* Are you cooking off-truck and bringing the food onboard to be heated? Are you cooking on-truck? As a mobile caterer, will you bring burners and other equipment that must be moved to each location? If you have a trailer or cart, where will you be set up and how often will you change locations? Do you shop for your ingredients? When? Where?

   Carefully think through this section. Much of it depends on what foods you sell, the size of your mobile vehicle, and whether or not you have (or are required to have) an off-site commissary kitchen. Walk yourself through the entire operation step by step to see if it works smoothly. Then write it down.

8. *Financial.* The goal here, with help from your accountant, is to make realistic projections based on researching similar businesses. Here you show the numbers and see where you will make profits—or not. This is a must-do section whether or not you seek a backer. You need to know your profit potential and how long it will take to start showing a profit after purchasing the vehicle and equipment. Also include a cash and balance sheet for a year to show a cash flow. Hint: Be conservative in your financial estimates.

9. *Financial requirements.* If you are seeking funding, include the amount of financing needed, based on the previous sections, to reach your goals. Detail how you will be spending the money you receive from investors. Again, be realistic,

research costs carefully, and indicate how much money you anticipate putting into the business venture yourself. Hint: You stand a much greater chance of getting investors interested or bank loan approval if you have invested your own money into the business.

Add any supporting documentation, which may include various financial reports, culinary awards, diplomas, or anything else that highlights your story and a business plan. You also want to make sure to have copies of the licenses necessary to run your mobile food vehicle. Do not try to dazzle prospective readers with hype; provide the real story of the business so that it is clear on paper how it will operate and when you anticipate making money.

Of course, this is a very basic business plan outline. Before you sit down to start writing, you need to do research and look at other business plans in books or online. Websites such as Bplans.com or a computer program such as Biz Plan Pro from Palo Alto software (paloalto.com) can be very helpful.

tip

Most cities, and many towns, now have apps that curate information about food trucks. Find the ones in your area and make sure you are listed with your menu, location, specials and so on. Many of these apps are free and allow you to update your listing as often as you want. Take advantage of this marvelous marketing tool and remain active by updating often.

What's On the Menu?

f you look at the food trucks, trailers, carts, and kiosks on the streets and at mobile catering menus, you'll find that almost anything edible can be served up street side. Of course the big question is: How practical is it? This may account for the lack of baked Alaska carts out there, but rest assured, someone is probably selling it on some street corner.

Planning Your Mobile Menu

Determining what to serve can be fun. But there are a lot of factors to consider when it comes to menu planning in the mobile food world. Here are a few:

- What do you know how to cook?
- What foods do you enjoy cooking?
- What foods are popular in your town, county, city, or region?
- What ingredients are easy to get from wholesalers, markets, or farms in your area?
- What foods are easy to transport to and from an off-site commercial kitchen?
- What can you prepare and/or heat up without much difficulty?
- What food(s) are ideally suited for your culinary expertise or allow you to try creative new recipes?
- What foods can customers easily carry around with them?
- What food(s) are potentially cost effective for you to sell?
- What foods are not being sold at 100 other food trucks, carts, kiosks, or mobile caterers in your area?
- What times of day will you be open for business? Breakfast? Lunch? Dinner? Late night? All of the above?
- Are you going to specialize in one or two foods with several variations such as pizza, tacos, or ice cream? Are you going to have a larger menu? Remember, a larger menu typically requires more space and may move you from a kiosk or cart to a truck or bus.

tip

As of 2014, there is a steadily increasing demand for cheap, freshly prepared food among 18- to 44-year-olds, according to the National Restaurant Association.

The Next Step

Unless you are buying prepared foods or have a chef providing you with foods, you'll want to plan your own recipes, work on them, re-work them, and have some taste tests. Consider your family and friends as your very own guinea pigs. Have parties, make a fun time of it, but get them to taste your foods and give you honest critiques. Don't be afraid of some criticism—better to receive it from friends and family than from food critics and customers.

Once you've found a few favorites, make sure you can master the recipes. Write them down for future reference. Next, try some variations on a theme. Most mobile food entrepreneurs spend several months, often while waiting for their truck to be retrofitted and their backers to fork over some startup money, experimenting with various menu items.

Another important consideration is the culture of the town in which you will be serving your foods. You may want to gear your menu to a younger audience in a college town or to a specific ethnic culture in a neighborhood made up of immigrants. In big cities, you may be able to select the neighborhoods that suit your style. You'll find neighborhoods where the gourmet foodies hang out as well as places where there are sports fans or the nightclubbers. Some areas are just right for tacos, and other areas have plenty of kids (and adults) looking for ice cream and cupcakes.

Menu Ideas

Now it's time to put on your thinking cap or chef's hat as the case may be. Below are some of the basics that foodies are finding at their favorite mobile food services. No, we don't want you to steal these culinary goodies, simply get some ideas for your own unique slant on popular menu items.

The Basics

- Sandwiches
- Wraps
- Salads
- Hot dogs
- Hamburgers
- Pizza

- Tacos
- Tortillas
- Gyros

It's hard to go wrong with basic food truck and food cart staples, especially if you put your own spin on them. The possibilities for sandwiches, hot dogs, burgers, pizza toppings, and salads are mind-boggling. How about Pulled Pork Mac and Cheese, a favorite of the college crowd who frequent Big Blue, the food truck at the University at Buffalo? You could think along the same lines as the MIHO Gastrotruck in San Diego, which featured a famous Stuffed Pork Loin Sandwich with all natural Duroc pork loin stuffed with bacon, local wild mushrooms, local braised greens, and walnuts, cranberry orange relish, Dijon aioli, gouda, and local rosemary focaccia.

If you prefer the more standard dog cart or burger wagon, why not opt for a hot dog with some flare like the We Be Weiners Chili Dog in Portland, Oregon, with chili, chopped onions, and grated jack cheese, topped with yellow mustard, ketchup, and relish. Or think along the lines of Seattle's Skillet Street Food with a burger of grass fed beef, plus arugula, bacon jam, and cambozola served on a soft roll.

If you want to stand out from your competitors, you'll want to try various slants on flavorful favorites. You can mix it up a little, but always serve some basic basics for the less adventurous crowd. Scout your competition, know your demographics, and get a feel for how innovative you can get. And remember, there's nothing wrong with a standard hot dog cart. They have been a staple on the street corners of New York City for generations. In fact, the Coney Island hot dog carts are still legendary. It works if your food tastes good!

One of the best things about going with the basics is that they are usually easy to purchase in quantity and easy to find. Food like hot dogs, gyros, and tacos are easy on-the-go foods that are especially popular with those looking to grab a quick lunch while being mobile themselves. Also consider buying from organic food vendors.

And don't forget breakfast. You can go with the more standard eggs on a roll, English muffins, blueberry muffins, and waffles, or be creative like Los Angeles's Buttermilk Truck with its red velvet chocolate chip pancakes or Hawaiian Bread Breakfast Sliders.

Gourmet Delights

- Lamb and beef specialties

> **tip**
>
> Shop around for the paper goods you will need and find plenty of storage space. Because they are not perishable, load up in quantity to get the good bulk rate on things like napkins, straws, and coffee stirrers. If you buy enough from a nearby warehouse, you should be able to have them delivered.

- Designer potatoes
- Duck delights
- Designer crêpes
- Escargot
- Crème brûlée
- Maine lobster rolls
- Shrimp sandwiches

One of the primarily reasons for the latest mobile food craze is that some of today's vehicles are serving up restaurant quality fine foods. While these eclectic dishes may not suit everyone's preference for a simple lunch, they do offer some upscale culinary delights at reasonable prices. In some cases, the trucks actually provide mobile tasting menus for established fine dining restaurants.

The keys to a gourmet food truck are having a gourmet chef and a means of transporting more temperamental flavors without stirring up trouble. A well-known chef can make a difference because she likely has a following. Jody Maroni's Sausage Kingdom was the first Kitchen Kingdom to serve gourmet sausages, including the Yucatan sausage with cilantro and chicken apple sausage. Jody was well known in the Southern California area long before gourmet food trucks hit the streets. So, when her truck emerged, she had an instant following. Likewise, when well-known chef Biagio Barone (who owns Biagio's Osteria, Zagats' top-rated Italian Restaurant in Connecticut), decided to open his gourmet food truck, GotChef, in Milford, Connecticut, people took notice. GotChef serves dishes like Sirloin Pinwheels (aka steak rolled with gorgonzola cheese and wild mushrooms) as well as Osso Bucco Milanese. Unfortunately GotChef may have gotten a little bit overly ambitious in a small market and, as a result, closed in 2012. Business is a numbers game and while the number of "gourmet" foodies in New York City, Chicago, or Los Angeles might provide a large enough market, it was not the case in Milford. Also, remember, gourmet food is a gamble since it typically appeals to a more sit down-fine dining crowd and doesn't present a strong potential for frequent visitors, where a taco truck may have people coming back for more two or three times a week.

As for taking foods on the road, sure, hot dogs, tacos and gyros travel well, while foods like flank steak marinated in lime, garlic, cilantro, and beer from Roy Choi's Match Truck may require a little more planning. But rest assured that nearly anything you or your gourmet chef can cook can be transported with enough due diligence on your part. The tricks are to find the right equipment and make sure you have the proper temperature to keep your foods at their best.

One of the keys to the success of the gourmet trucks has been touting a specialty that is fairly universal and draws attention. Fishlips Sushi truck in Los Angeles obviously has a specialty with plenty of choices as does Crepes Bonaparte, also in Los

Angeles, where you can start your day with the California Sunrise featuring avocado, crisp slices of bacon, sliced roma tomato, cheddar, and a fresh cracked egg or stop by later for a Spicy Apple Bottoms crepe with cinnamon apples, caramel, and whipped cream. Meanwhile, Sam's ChowderMobile in San Francisco serves incredible clam chowder and also offers things like Maine lobster rolls. Not a bad lunch choice. The size of your operation and the popularity of your specialty determines how much you can put on your menu. It's not about quantity; it's about quality. Many trucks, like Los Angeles's famous Grilled Cheese Truck, stick with a basic specialty and do it very well. This also holds true for running a cart or kiosk. You can be very creative within your setting.

A smaller venture only means thinking of unique ways to serve custom cuisine in a tighter space. Yes, you can certainly sell sushi from a cart or your own shrimp rolls from a kiosk. Keep in mind that while the food trucks are getting the press, the cart owners are keeping their costs way down. So don't be intimidated; there are plenty of options in the new street world of gourmet foods.

Ethnic Favorites

- Falafels
- Empanadas
- Egg Rolls
- Sushi
- Souvlaki
- Quesadillas
- Steamed Dumplings
- Kebobs

From Portland, Maine, down to Austin, Texas, and back up to Boston, ethnic food has changed the mobile food culture. Large markets are embracing authentic ethnic favorites while smaller markets are being introduced to new cuisines previously found in only a few establishments. "I had traveled a lot and missed things like the falafels and the street foods I had experienced in Europe. Selling falafels and kebobs in Market Square in Portsmouth, New Hampshire, was something new and they became very popular," says Michelle Lozuaway, who ran the Fresh Local truck in the small coastal town before becoming a restaurateur.

Much of the success found in ethnic fare emanates from the passion of the entrepreneurs. For example, the reason Curry Up Now went from one to five trucks in a few years, not to mention three restaurants and a catering business, in San Francisco is largely because the owners serve native foods from various parts of India, including a chicken tikka masala burrito. Another reason why Curry Up Now has long lines and may serve over 140 people an hour is because it changes its menu every day—not an easy task in the mobile food world. It is, however, a testament to the owners' desire to introduce native foods from all parts of India. If you're thinking Indian food and doing research, check out the India Jones Chow Trucks in and around the Los Angeles are, which serves what it calls the Frankie, an Indian Roti (flat bread), egg washed and rolled up like a burrito with chopped onions, tamarind chutney and a choice of lamb, chicken, beef, shrimp, or veggies. Again, the owners are passionate about their foods.

Sometimes, it's all in the fillings, as in the Chairman Truck in San Francisco that serves Chinese buns with fillings such as Muscovy Duck Confit Terrine or Mmmpanadas in Austin offering eggs, cheese, bacon, or chorizo fillings for breakfast. Variations on a simple theme can sell very well. Then there are the mixed ethnic options such as the famous Korean Mexican mix that made Kogi BBQ in Los Angeles the king of all food trucks and chef Roy Choi a foodie rock star. With some 130,000+ Twitter followers, the famed vehicle serves Calamari Tacos, Sweet Chili Chicken Quesadillas, and other ethnic blends that combine Korean barbecue with homemade tortillas and other wrappings that have tastefully paved the way for the food truck revolution.

And if you can bring a new ethnic flavor to your town or city, by all means go for it. Yvonne's Jamaican Food Truck in Manhattan is doing just that with Jamaican favorites like curried goat or brown stew chicken for only $6 to $9.

Desserts

- Ice Cream
- Cupcakes
- Donuts
- Brownies
- Cookies

Dessert trucks and carts carry those edible delights that make people smile. Whether it's cupcakes like the classic Devil in Disguise, a red velvet cupcake with cream cheese frosting, from the Flirty Cupcakes truck in Chicago or a Brussels Wafel from Wafels & Dinges in New York City good dessert trucks or carts can create a brand name very quickly. Freshly made cupcakes, cookies, and brownies are easy to sell from a cart or a kiosk because customers can easily carry one or a bag of several. They are also easy to transport. In this case, your success is based largely on the freshness of your products, even more than on original flavors. Donuts may be a slightly tougher to market because Dunkin' Donuts or Krispy Kreme are everywhere and hard to compete against.

Of course, ice cream is the definitive mobile dessert. We've seen the trucks for years, and hearing the music playing harkens most of us back to our childhood. In fact, Adria Shimada, who opened the Parfait Ice Cream truck in Seattle in 2009 as the first organic ice cream maker in the state, recalled that one of her reasons for opening an ice cream truck was to capture the good feelings from her youth. "I thought about America's inherent cultural nostalgia for the ice cream truck. Then I recalled my own fond memories of hearing the bells and whistles of the Good Humor man down the street, then getting this lovely treat. It was a warm and fuzzy experience," explains Shimada, who was determined to make homemade ice cream from scratch and now has a following of over 3,000+ followers on Twitter for flavors like her Butter Toffee Crunch and fresh Mint Stracciatella.

tip

Toppings: Because ice cream sales are very competitive, one way to stand out from the crowd is through innovative toppings. Creative toppings have included Pumpkin Butter, mochi and Captain Crunch, Ginger Syrup, Key Lime Curd, Fresh Berries and Saba, Nutella, and even Wasabi Pea Dust. Try getting that from Mister Softee!

Adria Shimada peers out from her popular Parfait Ice Cream truck in Seattle, Washington.

Like many dessert makers, Shimada has found that trying new and inventive flavors attracts a crowd, while simply making marvelous versions of standard favorites provides a mass audience.

While ice cream is certainly a fun food, the business needs to be taken just as seriously as that involving any other food. If you opt to make your own ice cream, understand that making it is a two-day, or more, process that needs to be repeated regularly and done very carefully. If you master it, you're past the first step to serving homemade ice cream. If not, buy manufactured ice cream and find creative and cost-effective ways of serving it—again, and think toppings. It's also to your advantage to offer various sizes, choices of cones or cups, sundaes, and other options.

Because ice cream is scooped and then served, and scoop size can vary, you need to be extra careful when determining your costs. Your profit will be based on how many scoops you sell and what you need to charge per scoop and per topping. If you are serving homemade, organic fresh ice cream, you may need to charge more. After all, you have to buy each ingredient.

Along with scoopers and other equipment, your most important onboard item is your freezer. You'll want a chest freezer with an adjustable thermometer. Whether you are making ice cream or serving known brands and all sorts of popular pops for the kids, you will want to serve high-quality products and find good locations.

In many parts of the country, ice cream business drops off significantly between November and March. If you can plan carefully, you might be able to shift gears from a cart or truck to an indoor kiosk at a mall, hotel, or in a theater lobby by renting one well in advance for a few months. However, such locations may already be occupied. Another option is to cater kids' parties during the cold months or sell your ice cream in pints or larger quantities and deliver in your area. Adria of the Parfait Ice Cream truck is doing just that in Seattle. When it's too cold to take the truck out, and she's not in her shop's she fills orders and delivers her homemade ice cream.

When selling ice cream, also consider selling gelato, sorbet, and other ice cream variations for the carb-conscious crowd.

Beverages

- Soda
- Coffee

> **tip** ⓘ
>
> **Don't Overdo It**
>
> "I make more than 20 flavors of ice cream, but only offer about six at any given time," says Adria Shimada. The idea is to make life simple so that you only need to make a few flavors at a time. Then you can provide your customers with some choices but not so many that they stand there causing long lines to form while making a decision. Remember, unlike an ice cream shop, your counter space is very limited.

- Tea
- Hot Chocolate
- Bottled Water
- Juices
- Lemonade

Typically bottled water, soda, and popular fruit drinks are easy enough to buy in quantity and make a profit. Hint: buy both regular and diet soda, tea, and fruit drinks.

The one variable is, of course, coffee. It can be an important item, so much so that many truck owners leave it to the nearby Starbucks to handle it or to those cart owners who sell just coffee or espresso.

If you sell coffee, you need to make sure it is freshly brewed on a regular basis. Bad coffee can be disastrous. You also need to offer various sizes, plus decaf and all of the necessary accouterments: milk, sugar, sweeteners, cream, creamers, and stirrers. Tea can be easier because it's hot water and a variety of tea bags, which may be herbal or regular. Hot chocolate is also relatively simple and inexpensive to carry. But java is still the king of hot beverages. You will have to scout around very carefully when looking for locations because Starbucks seems to be everywhere. Fortunately a coffee or an espresso cart has wheels. If you turn the corner and come face to face with a green Starbucks sign, you can relocate quickly. However, If you're near a college campus, you may also come up against competition from Starbucks' new coffee trucks. As of 2105, the coffee giant has begun making those overnight cram sessions a little easier for students by sending out Starbucks trucks to campus locations with most of the company's usual menu.

When it comes to coffee, espresso, or other hot beverages, the bar has been raised very high so you will need to work long and hard to match or top the coffee elite. There are some coffeemakers that have made the grade in the mobile world such as the New York's famous Mudtruck featuring a blend drip coffee, a strong brew with notes of cocoa and cherry.

> **tip**
>
> If you are buying coffee from wholesalers, consider major players such as, Specialty Java, or Caribu Coffee among other known favorites. Because coffee is so immensely popular, smaller companies do pop up, but they often disappear, putting the consistency of your product at risk. Popular brands such as Eight O'Clock Coffee and Safeway are also good bets. Look for a tried-and-true brand and, perhaps, also offer it with a twist.

> **warning**
>
> Fruits are perishable. Therefore if you are selling fruit juices, you'll need to buy the right quantities so you will not be wasting too much fruit and cutting into your profits. Keep a close watch on how much you buy and sell until you become very good at estimating your daily fruit needs.

tip

Taste before you purchase foods. Everyone will try to sell you on quality, but you're the one putting your reputation on the line. Find the brands you like or the growers whose foods are the freshest. Also make sure to read all labels very carefully and save at least one label from everything you sell. Customers today often ask if certain ingredients are in what they are buying, and you need to have the correct answers. If someone gets sick because of an ingredient in your food, you could get sued. Therefore, you need to know exactly what you are selling!

Cold beverages such a Hot Pink Lemonade with beet, lime, cucumber, and apple from the Green Pirate Juice Truck, also in New York, can be a welcome refresher, especially during the summer heat. And, if you can't afford a juice truck quite yet, for very few dollars, you can open a fresh juice cart.

As more and more people have begun focusing on healthier drinks, fruit juices have become a very popular alternative to soda. All you need to do is come up with a few recipes for fresh fruit juices, original or not, or buy concentrated juices at affordable prices. The more unique your juices, the more likely your cart can develop a following, especially if you are using farm fresh products. And don't forget that smoothies are also very popular.

Buying Your Foods and Ingredients

Sourcing, as they call it in the food business, is the process of getting your foods and other ingredients. Like a restaurant, you need to determine your potential volume and buy accordingly. You always need to be planning in advance to shop or receive orders so that you are never out of necessities. If you are cooking, make a detailed shopping list of ingredients. If you are buying food from wholesalers, know how much you need, how much you can safely keep fresh, and how much you can sell before any food goes bad. You are better running out of food on a busy day than selling something that isn't fresh. Determining the right quantities to purchase is usually trial and error.

Where to source your food, can be a factor in planning your purchases, schedule, and offerings.

tip

Don't take the first price offered, negotiate with distributors. Also, always punch up the numbers to make sure you can make a profit before striking a deal.

Wholesale Food Distributors

You can find plenty of food choices on the internet at sites like fooddirectories.com, foodprocessing.

com or wholesalegrocersdirectory.com, which offer directories of food and beverage suppliers. You can look up food wholesalers in your area or go directly to major ones such as Sysco (sysco.com) or Performance Food Group (pfgc.com).

One of the leading places to find local food is Agrilicious, a comprehensive Washington state based resource from Social Purpose Corporation, builds the farmer to family connection and encourages food buyers (from food trucks to caterers to restaurants) to support local food sources. From recipes to blogs to the background of organic farming to the local sources nationwide, there is a lot to learn from Agrilicious.

> **tip**
>
> Some wholesalers may ask to see your licenses. Have copies handy to show that you are indeed a licensed food seller when buying in bulk. It also helps to build good relationships with sellers that you like because they will know you will be back to buy again.

Manufacturers

Most major food manufacturers should be easily reachable and in many cases will sell you what you need or point you in the right direction so you can find their products nearby. Start with their websites. There are thousands of big companies to consider. There are also numerous small companies and niche providers that can supply you with a tremendous number of tasty options. From apples to zucchini, someone is ready with the food you need. As is the case when buying anything, compare prices along with quality as you shop.

Local and Regional Suppliers

If you start looking locally, you will find food distributors in your area.

Regional suppliers like Cheney Brothers in the southeast (Cheneybrothers.com) and Smart & Final (smartandfinal.com) handling the West Coast can also be very helpful if you are in their area of distribution.

Greenmarkets and Farmers Markets

A very popular option for some of the new food carts and trucks hitting the streets is to sell the healthiest versions of the basic food truck favorites by seeking organic farms and greenmarkets. You'll have to charge a little more to cover the slightly higher costs, but you'll attract the health-conscious crowd, and that's a big demographic in some areas.

Food shopping is a huge endeavor for Adria Shimada, who looks for all organic products to use when making homemade ice cream for her Seattle food truck and restaurants. "I get everything from a different distributor. Milk and cream come from a local certified organic dairy farm about 80 miles away, and I get eggs in another nearby town from another organic farm. All of my produce is real fresh produce, I don't use flavors or extracts. For my mint ice cream, I use real spearmint from a farm in Carnation, Washington," explains Shimada who scouted and tasted the food from many farms before finding her sources. Some deliver to her commercial kitchen, and others are found at farmer's markets in Seattle where farmers bring the wholesale quantities she needs.

Get to know area growers, talk to farmers and vendors at farmers' markets, and scout around carefully for whatever you need.

Food Cooperatives

When restaurateurs and/or mobile food owners order foods together in bulk quantities, they can save money. The larger the order, the better the discount. So if you can find some noncompetitive entrepreneurs, you can ask if they want to team up and place orders with you, which is how a food co-op is formed. A co-op is simply a group of individuals who come together for their mutual benefit, not unlike a credit union. You can look in your neighborhood for others interested in forming a co-op or, if you are interested in natural food co-ops (as well as finding plenty of information on co-ops), you can visit the Coop Directory (coopdirectory.org).

> **tip**
>
> If you have an iPhone or Android you can use the Locavore App to help you find fresh, local, farm-to-table ingredients from a growing network of farmers' markets. The application also lets you know about foods in season in your area. HarvestMark Traceability, NRDC's Eat Local, iFarmMarket, and Farmstand, with its international reach, are all free apps to help you find fresh foods. Urban Farming Assistant Start will even help you grow your own vegetables—can't get much fresher than that.

Shopping Clubs

BJ's Wholesale Club, Sam's Club, Costco, and other shopping clubs have become very popular in recent years as the idea of buying quality food in bulk has caught on. Restaurant owners shop at these clubs and so can you. Each requires a membership with an annual fee. You can then stock up on many items you need at good prices. Of course, you can also shop where the restaurant owners and their chefs shop—in places like Restaurant Depot and Jetro, which offer numerous choices at good prices.

What's Off the Menu?

While it's true that the food is what lures most people into this particular industry, your truck, cart, trailer, bus, or kiosk Is a key part of your business equation. In essence, it's your partner. It Is also what separates you from those brick-and-mortar restaurants, cafes, and snack bars that always seem to be nearby.

Along with mobility, the latest in technology provides you with a marvelous opportunity to compete with brick-and-mortar eateries. Smaller ovens, speedy convection ovens, mini-freezers, the latest in mobile generators, and a host of portable appliances make it possible to transport, cook, and serve foods almost anywhere. In addition, stainless steel counters and work stations, plus heavy duty cleaning products make it easier to meet health codes. You'll also find a wide selection of vehicles that are either built or retrofitted to your specifications. Gone are the days of struggling with a cart or truck that barely meets the needs of the food vendor. Today, you can hit the streets with the vehicle of your choice, or set up a state-of-the art kiosk in the busiest mall in town. You can also offer greater variety in food choices and grow a steady customer base thanks to mobile communication tools.

There are advantages to being mobile. For example, besides not having to pay the high startup costs and monthly rent, you also do not need as many people on your payroll. And if a restaurant is not drawing a crowd, it is stuck in its location. You, on the other hand, can always pick up and move. Being mobile means finding locations you like. As for caterers, being mobile means you are not sitting with an empty catering hall during the slower months. Instead you can always create new themes and focus on holiday parties (for any occasion) rather than worrying about how you are going to pay your rent.

Of course the downside of mobility is the many local rules and regulations that can limit your opportunity to sell. In most regions of the United States and Canada, your sales success is also limited by inclement weather.

Sure there are pros and cons to going mobile, but if you are considering taking the plunge, then you need to focus on a vehicle (or kiosk) that meets your needs. Vehicle choice depend primarily on:

- Size and scope of your projected business endeavor
- Food or foods you plan to serve
- How much you are planning to invest in the business
- The area(s) in which you will be operating
- Your financial goals and expectations

Carts

"Carts are like cars, you can build a VW or a Mercedes Benz," says Mike Boyd from Cart-King (cart-king.com), a major food cart seller that works with buyers to create the best cart for their individual needs. "The features you decide to include will depend on your needs and the state rules and regulations," adds Boyd.

Hot dog carts are typically pushcarts. They will have a grill, splashguard, hot and cold running water, two-basin sink, waste tank, plus a storage area for supplies and possibly an insulated storage area in which you can keep cold soda or bottled water.

Ice cream carts are typically pushcarts designed to hold ice cream vats, with a dipper well with running water, stainless steel pans or trays for toppings, display area, and storage compartments for cups, cones, etc. The latest in cold trays have replaced dry ice and remain cold during your sales day. They can be electrically charged during the off-hours.

"Food carts in the right locations can do $500 to $1,200 in business a day," notes Boyd, of the more successful cart owners.

Depending on your needs (and the local licensing requirements), you have carts that include:

- Stainless steel burners
- Propane tanks (and hook up) for power
- Power cord for indoor use or at fairs and other venues where electricity is available
- Display area(s)
- A stainless steel cooling compartment
- Three- (and even four) basin stainless steel sink: for running water, for food preparation, for washing your hands, and for cleaning utensils
- Hot and cold running water: uses a self-contained pump system with one tank for clean water tank and one for gray (or dirty) water
- Hot water heater for coffee or espresso (or tea)
- Various (locking) storage areas
- A removable hitch for pulling by car or van
- Rear lights and blinker lights for towing
- Stainless steel counter, including a small cash register or cash box
- A heavy-duty canopy
- Heavy-duty handles for pushing
- Space for signage
- Large-capacity ice bin for holding cases of soda with ice or other cold products
- Display oven for pizza, pretzels, and knishes
- Grill for heating foods
- Cold trays for ice cream
- Serving shelves
- Mechanical refrigeration

tip

Get a flattop grill. "Many carts today have flattop grills," says Mike Boyd of Cart-King. "They make it easier for people to branch out and try new things like stir fry foods using a wok. They are also easy to heat and can be used to make multiple dishes like break-fast foods or hamburgers."

▲

Ten Things to Consider When Buying a Cart

1. What features are included—do they meet your specific needs or not?

2. Ease of handling and comfort of handles or ease of hitching to your vehicle.

3. The weight of the cart. Is it too heavy to push? To tow?

4. How easy is it to secure everything so that nothing falls or breaks when moving.

5. Does the cart require assembly when you buy it? How easy/difficult is it to assemble?

6. The wheels. Do they lock? Make sure they are sturdy and not worn.

7. The height and width. A narrower cart can squeeze in tight spaces—but may not have enough space to meet your needs.

8. Can you set it up and break it down easily?

9. Does the cart feel sturdy and well constructed?

10. And finally, consider the style and design. You want it to represent the theme of your business.

- Water softening system
- Water filtration system
- LCD advertising screen options
- Locking caster wheels

Used Carts

A new six-by-three-foot food cart typically starts at about $4,000, but they can run up to $20,000 depending on the size, features, and quality. You can save a lot of money on a used cart. Just remember, you are putting your business on this vehicle, so make sure that it is in good condition. Like a used car, take it out for a spin or push, and make sure it is to your liking. Try shopping around. You can find used carts for $1,000 to $ 3,500, depending on wear and tear, size, and features. Look for a cart that was used to sell similar foods to those that you will be selling. After all, why convert a former ice cream cart to sell hot dogs? There are plenty of used hot dog carts available.

Kiosks

Food kiosks are generally used indoors in rented or leased spaces in malls, arenas, conference centers, hotels, airports, and similar locations. Larger, outdoor kiosks can be used at amusement parks. The kiosks themselves can run anywhere from $3,000 to $50,000 or more depending on the size and how elaborate they are. But the fees for a location can run you as much as $100,000 depending on where are doing business. Success for kiosks, like carts and trucks, is largely about location, location, location but in this case, getting one within a prime location can be costly.

It is important that you not only know the health codes and municipal requirements for food preparation and sales, but also the rules, regulations, and restrictions of the venue in which you will be selling. While kiosks generally do not have to deal with the limitations of the weather, you will probably have limitations imposed by the indoor location, especially hours of operation. If the mall stays open until 9 P.M., you obviously cannot stay open until 10 P.M. The same holds true if you are part of a food court. In addition, malls may specify that you have a design that fits in with their décor. They will also let you know what signage is and is not permitted, so make sure you meet the needs of the location before you buy, build, and/or retrofit a kiosk.

A stand-alone kiosk is typically good for serving simple offerings such as pretzels, donuts, cupcakes, and other items that need not be heated. Coffee is the one hot product frequently sold in kiosks. To cook in a kiosk, you need a ventilation system so you do not have smoke billowing into an indoor facility. For this reason, kiosks serving cooked foods tend to be restricted to foods court where both ventilation and electricity are available. While your costs will be higher (because you are renting space in the venue), you can make upwards of $2,000 a day at a kiosk in a busy location. You may also consider franchising an express kiosk from one of many major food chains. (See Chapter 11 on franchising.)

Along with many of the features found in food carts (listed above), a kiosk may include:

- Extended, often lighted, counter space
- More display space

warning

Unlike carts, trucks, and buses, you are unable to pick up and move if business is slow. Therefore, it is important that you do not let yourself be lured into a lease or a "discount" rental price in a bad location. Make sure you scout carefully to see how much foot traffic the area actually has. Also see if you have any competition. Even if you are the only pretzel kiosk in the airline terminal or local mall, you should ask about having a clause in the lease that no other pretzel kiosk can open up while you are in there, at least not on the same floor.

▲

- Larger and lighted signage
- Refrigerated cases
- Actual roofs rather than canopies
- More cabinets and areas for supplies
- More elaborate design

Food Trucks

When buying a food truck, you have two specific issues to consider:

1. The truck itself
2. The food preparation portion of the truck

Despite the urge to start retrofitting a truck before you even test drive it, the need to have a vehicle that can serve you over the long haul is very important. No matter how good your food is, nobody gets to taste it if your truck is broken down somewhere in a tunnel.

Depending on the size of the truck, the equipment necessary, the retrofitting, and whether you are buying new or used, truck costs can run from $15,000 to more than $100,000. They can also take anywhere from a few weeks to six months (or more) to retrofit properly. Try to get a good estimate of time required from whomever you hire to design your truck, then add a month to the timeframe.

Obviously, the advantage to a new truck is that you get a warranty, have it designed to your liking, and built to meet local regulations from the start. Also, everything is brand new. Of course, the other side to the equation is that it will cost you a lot of money. If you do not have financial backers, this can delay making a profit.

As a result, many food truck owners work from used retrofitted trucks. If you decide to buy a used truck, you should have a mechanic that you trust inspect the vehicle carefully. Before even thinking about food, you want to make sure the truck is in good shape to travel and carry your equipment on a daily basis. Kim Ima, owner of the Treats Truck of New York, which sells cookies, brownies, and other baked goods, found a used vehicle for sale on eBay in the fall 2006 and bought it for less than $20,000. Laurent Katgely, who owns the San Francisco French restaurant Chez Spencer, opened a food-truck business called Spencer on the Go! after buying a former burrito truck for $15,000. In fact, most of the food truck owners interviewed for this book purchased used trucks to start their businesses.

When buying a truck, you will need to consider typical truck issues, such as how well the truck handles, how easy it is to maneuver and whether it can accommodate the weight of the necessary equipment. Keep in mind that a heavier truck (typically

---

Three Key Concerns for Used Truck Buyers

1. *The Engine.* Have it checked out by a licensed mechanic.

2. *Space Issues.* Measure to make sure not only your equipment will fit, but that there will be sufficient room for one or two people to work comfortably.

3. *Is it Cost-Effective?* A used truck, retrofitted to meet you needs and health code regulations, should cost significantly less than a new truck.

---

over 26,000 pounds) will also require the driver to have a commercial truck driver's license.

Used trucks may come with some wear and tear, so you will need to check the truck out carefully. Make sure that everything works, from the sinks and freezers to the headlights and sound system, if there is one.

What to consider when buying a food truck:

- Does the truck handle well? Make sure the truck does not overwhelm you and that it is easy to maneuver.
- Is it easy to see behind you and alongside of you from the mirrors?
- Is there enough room to fit the equipment you want into the truck and still maneuver comfortably inside?
- Is the price within your budget? Are there financing options?
- What is the weight of the truck? A heavier truck (typically over 26,000 pounds) will usually require a commercial (truck) drivers license.

When buying a used truck:

- Check the year, model, and make of the vehicle as well as the mileage. You want to make sure you can find parts if necessary. You also don't want a truck that has significant mileage.
- Make sure the engine and all parts are in good condition.
- Determine if the truck is retrofitted to meet your needs and how much will need to be changed.
- What is the condition of the equipment? How much needs to be replaced? (Hint: Check to see that everything works, from the headlights and the radio to the sinks and food warmers.)
- Is there enough room to meet your specific equipment needs?

In addition to many of the features found in food carts, trucks may also include:

- Larger refrigerators and/or freezers
- More power through propane or a generator
- Additional food service or preparation equipment
- Additional cabinet and supply space
- Side serving windows and countertops

When searching for a truck, you might consider buying an inexpensive van, former postal truck, or a similar nonfood-related vehicle. A number of food truck owners have done this. The truck is retrofitted, which typically means removing any seats except those in the front, changing the flooring to something that is very easy to clean (and not slippery), and building a counter and window in the side of the vehicle. You will also need to install power via propane tanks or a generator.

tip

Whether you plan to cook on your truck, bus, or attached trailer, you must have a hood/fan system with a fire suppression device. If you are using gas, you must also include an automatic gas shutoff with the hood system. This equipment can be costly to install and maintain, so an off-site commercial kitchen, which comes with such equipment, can be a better choice. In fact, some cities require you to cook in an off-site commercial kitchen.

Mobile Catering Trucks

Mobile catering trucks are those hired to provide food for a party or gathering at a location of the client's choice. If your catering business is primarily transporting food and not serving it, you face less stringent requirements then if you are preparing and serving food. Along with the concerns about purchasing a good quality vehicle, you need to purchase the right truck for what you do. If transporting food from your kitchen to the location of the party or event is your number-one concern, then you need to focus on square footage, shelving, and ability to secure everything you are carrying. Of course you may need refrigerators, freezers, and/or warmers. If you are not serving from the truck, sinks and serving areas are not necessary, minimizing some costs.

Conversely, if you are actually cooking on site, you will need food preparation permits and licensing. Again, you have to determine if legally you can cook

tip

Measure all equipment carefully. You only have so much room in any vehicle or kiosk. Your designer can help you determine what fits, but you may need to add equipment or make changes. Measure, measure, measure.

on board your vehicle in your town or city. If you cannot, your other option is to bring grills and other equipment and cook in designated areas, such as places where barbecuing is allowed. More on mobile catering is found in Chapter 8.

A typical mobile kitchen includes:

- Cooking equipment with an exhaust hood
- Refrigerator
- Utensil and hand-washing sinks with hot and cold running water
- Service windows
- Stainless steel counters
- Roof windows with aluminum screens
- Prep tables and/or counters
- Multiple storage counters/sinks
- Propane tanks
- Emergency exit

warning

One of the biggest mistakes food truck owners make is overloading their vehicle. Trucks can only carry so much weight before they start having maintenance problems. Look for a truck that can accommodate all that you require. Your truck should be able to handle at least 15,000 pounds as the gross vehicle weight.

Bustaurants

Bustaurants are still fairly new. World Fare and Le Truc were the originals, breaking new ground and ruffling some feathers. Unfortunately both have since closed. Nonetheless, bustaurants, although rare, do continue. One of the hottest Bustaurants today, Food Fighters in even serves up a roast beef on Cuban bread with dipping sauce called the Dippitadydoo. To buy a Greyhound or a double-decker bus and retrofit it as a restaurant can cost upwards of $250,000. One must consider that to buy and retrofit the Food Fighters school bus had to cost a bit of money as well.

The concept of using the upper deck or part of the vehicle as a dining area is unknown in most towns, cities, and counties, forcing legislators to write new rules. Meanwhile, you will be subject to the same health department licensing rules and regulations of food trucks.

The novelty of the bustaurant is eating onboard. To accentuate that novelty, themes are also part of the "charm" of this new dining experience. Essentially anything you could put in a cart or truck can fit into a bus—and more—depending on local rules and regulations. You need to calculate and measure the space for actual dining, which means tables and chairs, but the number of diners you can have may be dictated by fire department regulations.

▲

While those with a lot of capital can consider the bustaurant as an exciting venture, there are some issues you have to deal with.

- Their success is still somewhat unproven. Because they are new, it is still not clear if they are a passing fad (literally) or here to stay.
- They require a driver or drivers that are comfortable handling a vehicle of this size and licensed to do so.
- There will certainly be parking issues. San Francisco's Le Truc was met with protests. Local authorities tend not to want buses parking all over town.
- The cost of maintaining a bus is significant.
- While some are greener than others, running on bio diesel, many environmentalists are not thrilled with the idea of having more buses on their city streets.

In high tourist areas, bustaurants seem to be popular thus far. They may become the next generation of mobile dining or remain as a novelty—time will tell. Most newcomers to the industry would be advised to follow them (literally if possible) to see how they do before jumping on board.

On the bright side, in many cities you would be among the first to have such a large mobile dining facility. While municipalities typically frown upon food preparation and even serving food while on the move, you can plot out an itinerary that has a different course at each of a few locations. You can also pick up customers and drive around before and after the dinner is served. Why not have your customers transported from the hustle and bustle of downtown to a romantic location, serve a romantic dinner, and then bring them back? With the right theme, atmosphere, and promotion, a bustaurant can be a unique and profitable business. But, be forewarned, it is a costly adventure.

Retrofitting

Adria's Parfait Ice Cream truck in Seattle was bought used from someone in Michigan who ran it as a traditional ice cream truck, selling packaged products. Adria makes homemade ice cream and had to customize the truck to meet Seattle health codes because she was actually scooping the ice cream herself, which is considered food preparation. "An ice cream truck or a cart selling packaged products doesn't need the same equipment, such as a hand sink on the truck, so my truck had to have sinks installed to meet the regulations," explains Adria.

Like most entrepreneurs, she carefully considered what she would need for her small truck and made a list. Designers typically work from the list you provide for retrofitting and make recommendations based on what you need in order to meet health codes. They can also help you with size and space issues, which are trickier than you might think.

Plan Carefully—Have a Design in Mind

Wouldn't you like to design your kitchen from scratch? Well here's your chance, sort of. The larger the vehicle and/or the more foods you are selling, the more carefully you will have to create, and review, your floor plan. Rule of thumb says keep it simple when starting out by serving only a few items or make one item (i.e., cupcakes or ice cream) with variations on the theme.

Your plan, whether created by hand or on a computer program, should outline the specific equipment you need and the easiest way to move around efficiently. For example, if you are selling pizza, you need a pizza oven, three-compartment sink, hot water system, beverage cooler, freezer, and prep fridges all mounted properly. You want sufficient counterspace, a multi-tiered heated display case, room for your cash register, a place for toppings, and storage for paper goods, cleaning supplies, and anything else you need to bring along, plus a propane fuel system to power most of the above. You also need proper ventilation, a serving window, and a fire extinguisher.

Clearly a coffee truck and a pizza truck will be designed differently, so you need to commit to a rough menu in advance. List the types of food you will sell and where you will need to store them, heat them, prepare them, and so forth. Include each item on your list (i.e., freezer, deep fryer, heat lamp, etc.). Then start deciding where each

Food Trucks Go Hollywood

In 2014, food trucks went Hollywood with the feature film *Chef*, starring Jon Favreau and Sofia Vergaa. The film zeroed in on a famed chef who had a major falling out with the restaurant owner (played by Dustin Hoffman) over what direction the restaurant would take and what they should serve a leading L.A. food critic (Robert Downey Jr.) After a melt down with the critic the chef (Favreau) leaves in a huff and ends up back in his hometown of Miami, where he discovers cubanos and decides to sell the popular sandwiches with yucca fries from a food truck. The film takes viewers through the hard work of retrofitting a truck and starting a food business. Favreau, his son, and his assistant (and close friend played by John Leguizamo) then take off across the country selling the sandwiches while incorporating local ingredients in cities such as New Orleans and Austin. His son, savvy on social media, spreads the word that they are coming to the various cities where they are a hit. While, somewhat Hollywood-ized for the screen, the movie successfully brought the food truck experience to a new audience while generating $45 million in sales and critical acclaim.

item would fit best keeping in mind work flow. You need room for food prep and then a place to plate and serve. If you are planning to do the job yourself, you need to first do the grunt work of cleaning out the truck thoroughly before you can even consider retro-fitting. Next you'll have a litany of considerations to address which includes:

- Measuring everything and marking where it should go.
- Finding an electrician to help make sure wiring is adequate.
- Framing the walls with aluminum.
- Cutting out your serving window.
- Installing your air conditioning unit.
- Insulating your vehicle for safety and to meet fire codes.
- Safely installing a propane tank complying to state or city regulations.
- Installing your generator in a ventilated area.
- Adding the interior hood to ventilate the vehicle.
- Having a plumber help you install your sinks.
- And, making sure that everything works!

tip

There are many cart, truck, and kiosk designers. Asking other mobile food vendors, doing a search on Google, or checking the resources in the back of this book can provide names of places. Many outfitters will take care of permits, insurance, and maintenance; and some include POS technology. Ask what is offered before selecting someone to be your designer.

Buying or Renting

Depending on the equipment and the size, a new food truck could cost you more than $100,000. Conversely, renting a truck will cost you about $3,000 a month (depending on the size and condition of the vehicle.) The obvious advantage of renting is the cost saving. As is typically the case, the downside of renting is that you cannot sell the truck one day. You are also held to the terms of the rental agreement. Another option is to start a business with a rented vehicle, see how it goes, and possibly buy the vehicle once you are familiar with it and have determined that you like being part of the mobile food business. Look for rentals with an option to buy.

Clearly, this is a very rough list of what goes into retrofitting a food truck. You can find more detailed retrofitting information by googling "retrofitting a food truck" online. Of course there are always a number of personal touches you can add and equipment that suits your needs.

Once you have worked with a designer to retrofit the truck, or you've done the job yourself, you will need to map out how someone will take a slice from a heated display, add toppings, heat a slice or individual pizza, get the customer's drink, serve the customer, and collect the money all in a fluid motion. Take your time to make sure the process works. It can be very costly to redo the infrastructure of your retrofitted vehicle once it is completed.

If you are buying an existing vehicle for the same usage, perhaps selling espresso just like the previous owner, it is advantageous to study how he or she ran the show. Of course, you may still want to make some minor changes to suit your needs.

Where Do Food Trucks and Carts Sleep?

Food kiosks typically stay at one location for the duration of the lease. As an owner, you need to make sure everything is carefully shut down at the end of the

Electrical Equipment

According to West Coast Catering, a company that sells catering trucks, electrical equipment in a food truck or mobile catering truck may include:

- ○ Interior fluorescent light fixtures with approved covers
- ○ Exterior light fixtures installed on service doors
- ○ Two-speed electrical fans in the exhaust hood
- ○ Electric water heater
- ○ 48-, 60-, 72-inch refrigerator
- ○ 110v electrical outlets
- ○ Electric generator: 2000 or 3000 watt output (quiet model)
- ○ 12-volt battery back-up system with battery charger
- ○ 15 amp. fuse block for fans and light fixtures

day. Often trailers shut down and remain at a location if it is permitted. For carts, trucks, and buses, however, the situation is usually different. Many cities require that a mobile food vehicle be parked in a health department–approved commissary parking location for both health and safety reasons. You will, therefore, have to find such a facility in your area. Rates vary from several hundred dollars per month to upwards of $1,000, depending on the local authority, the size of the vehicle, and what else is included besides just the parking. Facilities vary significantly. Some parking locations wash vehicles and sell fuel or propane. Many will let you use electricity to charge your equipment. Ask if there is a fee or it is included in your rental agreement.

It is also important to find parking that you consider safe. Many commissaries have security cameras and even someone on duty 24/7. You also want to know about the access if you plan to bring your vehicle back at off-hours. such as after serving the late night crowd leaving a ballgame at midnight or the nightclub crowd leaving the local hot spot at 3 A.M. A commissary that is not far from your commercial kitchen, if you are using one, is also a plus. Sometimes the same company provides both a kitchen and vehicle parking, though typically not in the same location.

Once again, bustaurants are charting a new course. Indoor commissaries often do not have the room for parking large vehicles. You may need to find outdoor parking lots that are deemed satisfactory by the Department of Health, so this issue is important to investigate before starting a bustaurant.

Taking Care of Your Vehicle

Nobody wants to miss a day of work because of a flat tire or engine trouble, especially if you are in the mobile food industry where your inventory is also at risk of being wasted.

Because your wheels are almost as important as your menu, although less tasty, you need to have regular check-ups scheduled for your vehicle. If not for your own good, you will need to do this to appease the people handing out your permits and renewing your licenses. Remember, vehicle inspection counts for a lot in this business.

Routine maintenance not withstanding, it is to your advantage to take a course in vehicle maintenance. It is also your responsibility to keep the owner's manual that comes with a new vehicle or at least check the manufacturer's website for additional information about a used vehicle. Chevy, for example, has troubleshooting information online, as do most other vehicle manufacturers.

To play it safe, you or your driver must be aware of the condition of the truck. The wear and tear of carrying heavy equipment on a daily basis can take its toll on your vehicle. Many food and mobile catering truck owners are so concerned about the food end of the business that they neglect their vehicles. Plenty of stories abound of those bad days when truck owners learned that the alternator did not work, the battery died (never depend on the battery to power food equipment), or the gas gauge was on empty or a bit below before you almost reached your destination.

Therefore, you must:

- Check recall announcements. Some recalls are more critical than others for keeping the truck in service. You can visit www.AutoRecalls.us for recall information.
- Pay attention to all engine warning lights on the dashboard and never ignore one that is lit.
- Keep an eye on the gas gauge.
- Check the engine oil frequently.
- Make sure all lights are working.
- Make sure the fuel tank is not leaking.
- Make sure your spark plugs are not worn.
- Make sure all connections in the engine are not loose or eroding.
- Check your tire pressure often.

It Started with Artisan Ice Cream Trucks in New York City

In 2008 the first two Van Leeuwen Artisan Ice Cream trucks hit the streets of New York City. Today there are six trucks selling everything from finest quality chocolate and vanilla ice cream to mint chip, cinnamon, hazelnut, and red currents blended with fresh cream.

The Van Leeuwen's have worked long and hard to modernize their business and expand. They have now added stores in Boerum Hill, Greenpoint, and Williamsburgh in Brooklyn, as well as in the East and West Village in lower Manhattan. They've even gone cross-country with trucks and new stores in Los Angeles proving that food trucks can lead to much more if give the customers what they want.

▲

- Make sure windshield wipers are working, and change the blades if they are getting worn down.
- If you hear a noise while driving and all food equipment is off, pull over, stop, and shut the vehicle off. When you start up again (assuming you can start up again), check under the hood if the sound continues to see if you can tell where it is coming from. Unless you have taken a troubleshooting course and know what to do, have the engine looked at by a mechanic as soon as possible.

Your commissary may offer some help with an available mechanic. If not, find someone you can trust. Also keep in mind that some national parts chains offer free diagnostic testing. Such testing can identify a problem.

Cart owners should not think this section is only for larger vehicles. While you will not have engine problems to worry about, wheels need to be in good shape at all times. Lights on the back of a vehicle being pulled are also supposed to work. In short, take the time to examine the cart carefully and make sure that all working parts are in good order. You will also very likely be required to park your cart in a specified area. In some cities, like New York, there are trucks that can be rented which take several carts at the end of a working day and transport all of them to a garage where they will be safe and sound overnight. Remember, your business is riding on your cart, so take good care of it.

Can I
Park Here?
Licenses, Regulations, and Points of Sales

Before you finish putting your menu together, building your perfectly retrofitted cart or truck, setting up your kiosk or hitting the road on a fabulous bustaurant, you need to get your licensing in order. While that's not one of the more exciting aspects of your entrepreneurial pursuit, it's one of the most important. It is, in fact, the overall commitment to more stringent health codes and sanitary regulations that have paved the way for food vehicles to generate such a mass following. The knock against food carts and trucks has long been that they were neither clean nor sanitary. Now, as that widespread perception changes, foodies and nonfoodies alike can enjoy their fare with confidence that those running the business are doing their utmost to meet, and surpass, sanitary requirements.

Licenses and Permits

It would probably take several volumes to list and explain the numerous permits and licensing requirements because each state as well as most cities and even counties have their own. However, there are many universal concerns that need to be addressed. Typically, your local department of health will have the information you need. Therefore, you can get started by looking up the local health department online or in your local Yellow Pages and calling to inquire about the necessary requirements.

The state or city will have specific requirements that must be met depending on your mode of operation. If you are selling prepackaged foods, you are not considered a food handler and may have less stringent requirements than if you are actually preparing foods or even scooping ice cream. As long as food is unwrapped, you are typically considered to be a food handler and must meet specific regulations. While your cart or truck designer will not know the nuances of each city's requirements, they can usually help you meet health standards. Before you can hit the road, health inspectors will inspect your vehicle. What are inspectors actually looking for? In Washington, DC, for example, an inspection is conducted to verify the following:

- Proof of ownership, proper identification, and license (of the vehicle)
- Proof of District-issued Food Manager Identification Card
- Food purchase record storage and record keeping
- Depot, commissary, or service support facility meets vending unit operation needs
- Copy of license for the service support facility and/or a recent inspection report be presented

Food vehicles are typically inspected at least once a year by a health department inspector, sometimes

tip ⓘ

There are nearly 20,000 separate licensing jurisdictions in the United States. Each has its own particular licensing requirements. Getting in touch with the right one(s) and finding out exactly what forms you need and how to submit them can be time consuming and tedious—but, it's part of business. Dedicate at least three days to locating and filling out forms.

randomly. The inspector checks to see how food is stored so that it does not spoil and that it is kept at the proper temperature. All food equipment as well as sinks and water supplies are checked. Commercial kitchens and garages in which food vehicles are kept are also inspected frequently and can be given high fines if they do not meet health and fire codes. Some have been shut down because of too many violations. Likewise, trucks and carts have lost their licenses over repeated violations.

Take New York City

One of the owners or partners of the intended food vehicle must have a mobile food-vending license with a photo ID badge. Once that is received, a Mobile Food Vending (MFV) Unit Permit is issued to the individual or business that wants to prepare and sell food from a mobile vehicle. After an inspector from the Department of Health and Mental Hygiene (DOHMH) conducts an inspection of the vehicle and it passes, the permit is affixed to the vehicle.

According to the NYC DOHMH, the number of MFV Unit Permits that may be issued for use on public space is limited by law. At present there is a very long waiting list, so getting a permit can take years. Those interested in obtaining a public space permit may only apply for one when DOHMH notifies them that their name has come up.

To work at street fairs or special events, people need to apply for a Temporary Food Service Establishment permit. A Restricted Area MFV unit permit can also be obtained to operate on private property or in a commercially zoned area.

Upgrading the Rules and Regulations

Keeping abreast of the latest changes in the rules and regulations in your city and/or state is very important. In New York City, the DHOMH, in recent years, has made changes to rules to improve sanitary practices in an effort to decrease the possibility of food-born illnesses. There is also an increased effort to clamp down on black market permits and the hiring of illegal immigrants. In New York City, not unlike other cities, there are also ongoing rule changes regarding the length and width of trucks and carts.

Whether it's a matter of keeping up with new rules and regulations or forgetting to adhere to the current ones, the New York City Courts still deal with nearly 60,000 vending cases every year with average annual fines totaling $433 per vehicle.

▲

Keep in mind that permits need to be renewed. Renewal applications are mailed to the last known address of the permit holder as the permit nears expiration, so remember to update your address should you move.

One way entrepreneurs have gotten around the problem of being unable to get a license from the city is by teaming up with those who already have licenses and including them in their business. They also may rent vehicles from those with licenses, which is technically illegal. Buying a license on the black market can get you arrested. Needless to say, nobody talks very much about licenses in the Big Apple.

Playing It Safe

To be on the safe side, it is highly recommended that you check with the proper regulating agencies in your area regarding specific requirements for your vehicle. You should also get into the habit of being as sanitary as possible from the planning stages forward. For example, food preparers today are required to wear disposable food preparation gloves—you can buy a box of 1,000 for less than $15 on Amazon.com. Foods should be wrapped or kept in sealed containers unless they are being heated or served. Sauces should be served in individual portions in disposable containers or in pour squeeze bottles. All foods that require refrigeration should be stored at proper temperatures. Proper refrigeration is extremely important because the last thing you want is to serve food that has gone bad. A bad reputation and/or lawsuit can ruin your business. Your freezer should be enclosed with an approved thermometer readable from outside the unit. In a truck or trailer, you are also required to have an adequate ventilation and/or air conditioning system that is able to maintain the interior ambient temperature within the proper temperature range of the refrigeration equipment.

As for retrofitting your vehicle, you'll want to start with the must-haves to meet inspection requirements in your municipality. You'll want to make sure that everything retrofitted into your vehicle is easily washable, from the floors to the walls to the preparation and serving areas. Use smooth, easily cleanable surfaces. This is why stainless steel is popular for equipment and commercial grade linoleum for floors. Also, doors and garbage can covers (all covers, for that matter) need to

tip ⓘ

Don't leave cracks or crevices when outlining your truck design. The more you can streamline the truck so that insects or vermin have no dark areas in which to hide, the better off you will be. Counters should be continuous. and storage should go to the floor. In fact, light colors are advised, and in some cities/counties they are mandatory.

be tight fitting. Trash receptacles need to be lined with proper trash bags. From major food preparation equipment down to proper dispensers for napkins, stirrers, and plastic utensils, you need to address everything in the vehicle or kiosk from the safest, most sanitary perspective possible. The department of health in your area will spell all of this out in detail.

Other things health departments frown upon include:

- Rust
- Wood surfaces
- Jagged or sharp edges
- Anything that is obstructed from cleaning
- Uncovered plastic utensils for customers
- Lack of splash guards around hand-washing sinks

If you are operating a full kitchen on your vehicle, you will have additional state and/or local requirements. Most retrofitters and kiosk, cart, and truck sellers can help you through the process. Bustaurants essentially follow the rules for trucks and will very likely have new health regulations as they become more popular.

Application Process Prerequisites

Of course, before you can even apply for most licenses, you need to have your own information readily available. While local authorities vary in what they require, you will typically need to provide your:

- Mailing address and proof of address
- LLC, partnership, or a stamped copy of corporation papers
- Social Security number or tax identification number
- Valid photo ID
- Valid driver's license (for at least one person involved in the business)
- A list of all operators of the vehicle
- State certificate of sales tax
- Business license(s) and/or certificates as required by state, city, or county

These are some of the basics that may be required. Double- and triple-check with the licensing authority before showing up without one of the many necessary documents. In some areas, you may need to get a license or permit from other agencies, such as environmental agencies or local fire inspectors, particularly if you are operating a mobile kitchen.

Business Permits

Don't forget that with all the food service permits and meeting the stringent health requirements, you may also need to get the necessary business licenses in your city or county. City hall or the county clerk's office can usually point you in the right direction. Fees for business licenses are generally under $100. You can also go to your local city hall website to get appropriate licensing information. Licenses usually have renewal dates and there are late fees, so keep renewal dates on your calendar.

If you are doing business under the name of the truck or company, you will need a DBA (Doing Business As) certificate. This indicates that legally you are doing business under a fictitious name.

In addition, in most states business owners are required to register their business with a state tax agency and apply for certain tax permits as a seller. You may need to apply for a state sales tax permit. Consult your local tax office or check the IRS website (irs.gov). And if you are hiring employees, make sure to get an Employer Identification Number or EIN (aka a federal tax ID). The nine-digit EIN is important because it allows you to identify your business on government forms and official documents. Your federal tax ID not only makes the folks at the IRS happy when you file tax returns but also can be used in place of your personal Social Security number when you need to show business identification, thus keeping your Social Security number off of a lot of forms. Even if you are not hiring employees, you will need an EIN number if you have incorporated. The IRS makes it very easy to apply for EIN numbers and explains what you need to do on its website, irs.gov.

While most mobile food businesses are not incorporated, one reason to consider incorporating is to protect yourself personally from liability. If someone gets sick or injured and decides to sue you, she can sue the corporation and not go after your personal assets. While you may not be completely protected, it does put a layer of separation between you and your business. Incorporation primarily means filing a lot of papers and maintaining more stringent records. USA.gov has plenty of information on incorporating (usa.gov/Business/Incorporate.shtml) as does Nolo.com (nolo.com) and Learning Center at the Company Corporation (incorporate.com). Of course you should first consult with your attorney to see if such a move, or forming a LLC (limited liability company), is right for your business.

> **warning**
>
> It is of the utmost importance that if you have any employees, you keep records of them on the books and stick to the schedule of tax withholding payments. After all the time and effort you have put into opening your food business, you would hate to be shut down because the IRS finds out that you are hiring people and not following the tax laws for your employees.

Vehicle Licensing

Don't forget that vehicle permits and inspections are vital to your business. Food not withstanding, if you're driving a vehicle you will need to have proper vehicle registration. Carts and trailers may also need to be registered. Make sure you check with the Department of Motor Vehicles in your state to find out exactly what you need in your area, and stay on top of renewals. In addition, broken tail lights and other such problems need to be addressed prior to an inspection.

You need to have commercial plates on your vehicle. In most cities and states you also need a commercial driver's license if you are operating a vehicle over 26,000 pounds. Check the vehicle weight requirements in your state. Visit the Federal Motor Carrier Safety License Administration (fmcsa.dot.gov) for more information.

Zoning, Parking, and Other Considerations

Towns, cities, and counties have zoning restrictions, designating commercial and noncommercial zones. While you may be mobile, you can't park just anywhere. Most areas limit food trucks, trailers, buses, and carts to specific locations. A list of where you can and cannot park should be available from the county clerk—be persistent because you want to avoid parking tickets. In some places, you may also have to adhere to two-hour parking restrictions and (believe it or not) pay for parking meters—yes, even carts. Having to adhere to strict parking rules and being subject to parking violations is one headache kiosk owners can avoid.

Try not to dodge the local police because they will catch on and make your life more difficult. It's advisable to stay within the guidelines and befriend local authorities (give a cop a donut—just kidding!). However, if you play fair and establish a good rapport, when you do accidentally park in the wrong place or overstay your welcome, they may be more lenient.

Also be careful to park as close to the curb as possible—and never double park. You should also find out about other, lesser-known parking restrictions. Contact your local Department of Motor Vehicles or look for a local website online with city or town ordinances. For example, some municipalities have laws stating that a food truck or cart cannot park within a school zone or within X blocks from a school during school hours.

Alcohol or No Alcohol? That Is the Question!

You cannot sell alcohol from a mobile food vehicle. If you try to do so, you can lose your license. What you can do is look for a location for food sales within a reasonable (and allowable) distance of a neighborhood bar selling alcohol and promote each other.

As for an indoor kiosk, you'll have to consult your local laws as they may allow the sale of alcohol in some counties. In Pennsylvania, for example, automated wine kiosks drew a lot of attention when introduced in the summer of 2010. A year later, the Turkish Taco Truck was New York City's first food truck to serve alcohol and other trucks were quick to follow suit. Little by little laws are changing in some states but not others. As of 2014, mobile food vehicles in California and Texas could not sell alcohol. That being said, in California, catering trucks hired to work an event, not unlike a caterer for an indoor party could sell alcohol. Study the laws carefully in your state and/or community.

Then there are the store and restaurant owners that do not like your presence and will call the cops on you if you get too close to their businesses. At local town meetings these business owners (paying property taxes) are often heard from before food truck owners. In fact, Raleigh, North Carolina, banned food trucks from parking on the city's streets!

On the flip side, however, Eric Weiner of FoodTrucksin.com points out that the new founded popularity of food trucks, in many cases, has drawn business to local stores. In fact, some truck owners work out deals with stores to hand out coupons to customers waiting on line for food. Retailers can reciprocate by also letting customers know when the food truck will be in front of their location. Food and shopping, it's a combination that can benefit both parties.

Restaurant owners obviously do not want competition in front of their establishment. Of course, most food truck drivers get it and don't want to make trouble. Scott Baitinger of the Streetza pizza truck, in Milwaukee, Wisconsin, notes that there are not many stringent parking requirements in that city for food trucks, but says he simply would not park within

> **tip**
>
> If you team up with a noncompetitive business owner, you can both benefit by drawing business to each other. Look for someone who would benefit from your demographic audience and visa versa. Then come up with a cooperative marketing idea.

500 feet of a pizza parlor. Other food truck owners have made similar statements. Of course, the battles continue. In Chicago, Holly Sjo, owner of the Cupcake Counter, a small brick-and-mortar shop, called the police when she spotted the popular Flirty Cupcakes truck parked too close to her business. Chicago city ordinances prohibit parking within "200 feet of a restaurant and 100 feet of a business offering a similar service." It can lead to a ticket. Some business owners complain that food trucks accumulate parking tickets and just write them off as a business expense. While this is not the norm, trucks that are piling up tickets can make more trouble for everyone as city officials and business owners then work for stricter laws. In fact, it has been proposed in some areas that a certain number of tickets could result in the truck owner having his or her license suspended.

On the other hand, as Baitinger points out, his truck has gained a following and owners of some businesses such as nightclubs want the truck nearby to draw business to their establishment. Since food trucks have gained their own following, business owners have continued their love hate relationship with them. A popular, well-placed food truck can be useful by drawing customers to the right establishment. One of the ways in which the famous Kogi BBQ truck in Los Angeles gained such a huge following was by giving out free food samples to bouncers at the nightclubs who would in turn let the patrons know about the great food right outside.

Location, Location, Location

Your locations will play a major factor in your success. Your decisions on where to park for business purposes will depend on several key factors. First, you have to consider where you are allowed to park by law. Next, you want to ask yourself where in those areas can you find the customers that would like your foods and/or beverages. You also want to consider the prime hours for each potential location and, of course, the competition. Keep in mind that even if you've found the perfect lunch location on the map and you are allowed to park there, you may also find 19 other food carts and trucks lining the streets. As more food trucks appear on the streets of major cities like New York, Los Angles, and San Francisco, it becomes much more difficult to find prime locations.

Twitter has become a very useful tool for communicating with your foodie fans. They can guide you to where they are waiting and you can let them know where you will be. Twitter has been most effective at letting foodies know that their favorite truck is in its usual place and Instagram has added food photos to whet the appetite of the fans. And yes, Facebook is still a great place to keep in touch with your fans. Your goal should be, as it is for most mobile food vendors, to find a few regular locations, or in the case of some vehicles such as Mmmpanadas in Texas, one prime location. However, this is not as easy as it sounds. So what are food cart and truck drivers to do?

Some places to consider parking are:

- *Office parks.* Find out if food trucks are allowed to park and during what hours. If you are lucky enough to find an office park without much competition, stake a claim, or get a permit (if necessary) from the renting or leasing company to park there regularly. Breakfast and lunch hours should be your primary time slots.

- *Empty lots.* If you can find out who owns the property, make an offer to pay to park there on a regular basis. You can propose a flat daily rate, a percentage of your sales, or both. Such an agreement can benefit both parties and give you a chance to establish yourself. Of course you need to find a lot where there is enough foot traffic to make it worthwhile.

- *Shopping districts or malls.* You may or may not be allowed to park on a public street alongside the stores. Public streets are governed by local traffic laws. That being said, storeowners have a lot of say. Know your local ordinances. You may, however, be able to park near the parking lots or on an adjacent corner to a mall entrance. Malls will likely require you to have a permit to park on their property—inquire within the mall. Established shopping areas may have little room for you to park, but newer areas, recently opened for business, may give you an opportunity. You may, however, have some growing pains along with the storeowners.

- *Popular tourist locations.* The tourist crowd is often a great demographic. However, the competition can be fierce near well-known attractions. Sure, you will find food carts around Central Park in New York City, but many have established themselves in specific locations, making it nearly impossible to break into their territory. In some cases, you may need to pay for the privilege of parking at a prime tourist attraction, and it can be pricey.

  You can also look for the opening of a new museum, gallery, theater, arena, visitor's center, or any place that has just been added to the list of must-see places in your city.

- *Sports venues.* You may need permits to get close to an arena or stadium. However, if there is street parking for ticket holders, you can usually try to get on a street or a major roadway leading to or from the facility. Know which teams play where, and get a schedule in advance so you don't find yourself outside a football stadium in May.

- *Festivals and events.* "We take the truck to local events like Market Square Day, which brings in like 80,000 people, which is a lot for a town of 25,000," explained Michelle Lozuaway when she and her husband ran Fresh Local in Portsmouth, New Hampshire.

Events and local festivals can be an important part of food truck owners' plans. Event organizers have, in recent years, also started reaching out to popular food trucks to bring them in, knowing that they have followings of their own and can help promote the event. It is important, however, for food truck owners to plan well in advance (sometimes over a year ahead) to get booked at an event, especially if it's an annual, popular gathering.

> **warning** ⚠
>
> If you find a marvelous location in a popular food truck/cart town and over a number of days see no other food vehicles, chances are there is a reason. Sometimes things are too good to be true. Check this location out carefully before settling in. Chances are you can't legally park there, so be ready to move quickly.

- *Food truck festivals.* Not only do festivals attract food trucks but food trucks are now featured at festivals with music and various activities as the supporting players. From the Gourmet Truck Food Festival in Del Mar, California, featuring over 50 food trucks from the Los Angeles and San Diego areas to the annual Chicago Food Truck Festival to the massive 200 truck food festival in Tampa, Florida, dubbed the World's Largest Food Truck Rally ever, there are a growing number of events that you can travel to as a featured act. There are fees to participate and such festivals fill up fast, but they are a growing aspect of the industry and one to incorporate into your plans.

- *Food truck parks.* SoMa StrEat Food Truck Park in San Francisco is one among a growing number of outdoor food courts created by food trucks. Like the festivals, you need to plan ahead to be part of the fun, but in this case it is a year round place for foodies to enjoy.

- *Conferences and conventions.* As is the case with festivals, if they are annual events, they are planned well in advance. Get to know where they are staged and lease your space well in advance or find a place on a public street that leads to the conference or convention center.

- *Parks and beaches.* You need permits to park in a park or on beach property. Check with the local parks commission to see if you can get such a permit and at what cost. Carts may have the upper hand here because they take up less space. One of the Van Leeuwen Artisan Ice Cream trucks became a fixture in New York City parked by the former Tavern on the Green restaurant location in Central Park, thanks to a parks department permit and the okay by the owners of the restaurant property.

- *Bus and train stations.* If there is room, by all means consider these as busy locations where people may be hungry. Again, you have to know where you can

When to Re-Apply for a Business License

Even if you are up and running, you may need to re-apply for business licenses if you:

○ Incorporate

○ Add more carts, trucks, trailers, buses, etc.

○ Add catering clients outside of your town or city

○ Change your mode of operation in a major way, such as going from a hot dog cart to a pizza truck.

Check with the various licensing departments to make sure you have the additional licenses when making major changes to your business or to your vehicle. For example, if you upgrade from a smaller truck to a larger (heavier) one, you may need a commercial driver's license.

park, so inquire. Often taxis and buses have specific places in which they can park and you can get ticketed if you are in their way. Also, get an idea of which hours will see the most foot traffic.

- *College campuses.* Off campus, public streets may be good for parking. However, unless it is a commuter school, you may not have a lot of traffic. To get on campus for a few hours a day, you need to get a permit from the school, and that may be difficult depending on the institution and its policies. Some schools, such as the University of Buffalo, have their own food trucks, as mentioned earlier. Others will be home to the Starbucks trucks. If you cannot get onto campus on a regular basis, you may be able to secure a spot when there are major school events, such as football or basketball games. To be on the safe side, ask about the specific rules of the school, regarding parking, trash removal. and so on.

- *The business district.* Serving lunch in the middle of a busy business area can be terrific. However, in some cities, like New York, it's next to impossible to just slip into the mix without angering the competition (and you don't want to do that). Again, look for developing areas. Read about companies moving downtown or uptown or to a part of town that is now being built up or re-zoned for commercial use. Try to stake a claim in an up-and-coming area. You may struggle at first, as do many new businesses, but in time you may be the king of the hill.

Learning all about parking rules and regulations in your city and finding the best potential locations for your business takes due diligence. Even once you have found a few locations to your liking, keep on scouting around. Parking rules and regulations, as well as local ordinances, change often, so a good location one month may be gone the next. Also, note that as the seasons change, some locations become less viable, such as your great spot by the beaches on the Jersey shore, which will not be so great in the fall or winter months. So come up with other plans.

Scouting Around and Staging

Of course the most business, more than 50 percent for food carts and trucks, comes from streetside customers. To find local places to set up, you want to do some reconnaissance prior to setting out with your food truck. Then, once you find a prime location, study the hours and get to know when there is enough foot traffic to make it worthwhile. If you find a good location, you may decide to send a "staging car" or two, to park and grab prime real estate while you are loading your truck to drive over. This is your own means of saving a space and keeping competitors at bay in a very competitive business. If parking is legal, you may park your car in the space overnight.

Be careful when breaking into the business. Remember, you are the newcomer on the block. Some of your competitors will be happy to share, especially if your businesses compliment one another, such as a beverage cart and a pizza truck that does not sell beverages. However, many mobile food business owners are very territorial. You don't want to invade someone else's territory. Scott Baitinger of Streetza suggests that you get to know some of your local city council members and store or restaurant owners before selecting your regular location. Neighborhood associations and the local chamber of commerce can also be helpful if you befriend them.

Lending a Helping Hand

In early 2010, many mobile food vehicle owners sent nonperishables and money from their business endeavors to help the people affected by the earthquake in Haiti. Many mobile food vehicle owners have also been front and center during a local crisis or fundraising drive. New York City food truck owners, for example, stepped up and provided outreach after superstorm Sandy ravaged parts of both New York and New Jersey in 2012. Other food truck entrepreneurs have provided food during disaster relief. Being part of a fundraising drive is also a marvelous way to become part of your community. Food carts and trucks have also provided foods to those in need.

In New York City, The Woman's Housing and Economic Development Corporation (WHEDco) has been a leader in community development in the South Bronx. Along with being home to four commercial kitchens, the organization has brought food carts into the neighborhood.

"Our green carts project is designed to bring fresh vegetables to areas that otherwise do not usually have such produce readily available," explains WHEDco President Nancy Biberman, who founded the organization in 1991 after working for many years in an effort to clean up and help rebuild the Bronx. "The green carts is an initiative that was started by the Department of Health in response to concerns about communities that were in need of fresh produce," adds Biberman. It was also started to help boost employment in an area with significant unemployment.

Kerry McClean, who serves as Director of Community Development at WHEDco, is excited about the green carts and their continuing success, saying that the program, which includes 166 green carts in low-income neighborhoods throughout the city, "was ingenious," and she wants to see it continue to grow. The project is serving both purposes of providing jobs and bringing fresh produce to areas devoid of such foods.

The Work Environment

Commercial Kitchens, Cleaning, and Hiring Help

I n all mobile food businesses, you need to be comfortable working on your feet, sometimes for long hours and typically in tight quarters. Standing with a food cart or inside a catering truck in hot weather can get uncomfortable. From a personal hygiene perspective, you'll want to make sure you use deodorant before you start the day and wear sweatbands as needed. Make sure you have a means of keeping yourself cool in the heat of summer. Set up canopies or umbrellas to minimize the heat if you are operating a cart in a sun-drenched area.

As most food business entrepreneurs will tell you, the joy of your job is seeing satisfied customers enjoying your food. Nonetheless, the daily routine can be very tiring with its shopping, food preparation, cleaning, finding your location(s), serving, cleaning some more, returning your vehicle to its home for the night, cleaning some more, and perhaps doing truck repairs. Then there is the business paperwork that needs to get done. Yes, there are a lot of activities that may be part of any given day.

Although you will often be busy whether you are in a kiosk or a bustaurant, you will have slow periods when customers are not lining up. You may want to develop an affinity for reading, although chances are you will likely find something that needs to get done. Most mobile food entrepreneurs agree that there is always something to clean or fix or someone to reply to on Twitter.

The Commissary or Commercial Kitchen

Many of you will spend a lot of time in your commercial kitchen. Most jurisdictions require that you have a commercial kitchen if you are cooking food, rather then just heating up food or selling prepackaged foods. The commercial kitchen goes hand in hand with laws preventing you from cooking food at your home or in your vehicle. In the trade, such a commercial kitchen is known as a commissary. Like your vehicle, your commissary kitchen needs to maintain health code standards, which are not unlike those of a restaurant kitchen. These will be spelled out by the local health department. Typically, health inspectors look to make sure food is handled safely and stored properly (at proper temperatures), avoiding problems like salmonella or food poisoning. They also want to make sure that preparation tables and other surfaces can be thoroughly cleaned to prevent bacteria growth. Proper ventilation is also very important. The overall responsibility of making sure the commercial kitchen is up to code is that of the kitchen owners and manager. However, they will pass along their rules to you so that you can help maintain a clean kitchen for all parties concerned.

When renting a commercial kitchen, equipment should typically include:

- A commercial oven
- A large six-burner range. Gas can be cheaper than electric. Convection ovens are popular because of their speed and ability to heat more evenly.
- A microwave oven
- A rotisserie oven

- A flattop grill
- A commercial hood—make sure it was installed by a professional
- A commercial refrigerator—larger is usually better for professional needs
- A walk-in cooler
- A freezer—upright, chest, or walk-in
- A three-part stainless steel sink
- A large dishwasher
- Preparation tables that are durable and easy to clean
- A three-speed mixer with electric lift
- A deep fryer
- Stainless steel cabinets—add as many as you need
- Fire extinguishers—for businesses, not a small residential one
- Rubber floor mats
- Cleaning supplies and rags
- Hand soap and/or sanitizer dispenser
- A mop sink

Renters may need to provide additional supplies and equipment such as those listed below.

- Various pots and pans
- Bowls, plates, and baking sheets
- Utensils
- Ladles, tongs, and spatulas
- Strainers
- Various small appliances

These are just some of the many items found in commercial kitchens. You can bring additional equipment. Inquire about having a place to store whatever you bring so that you do not have to schlep it back and forth with you. In many commercial kitchens, storage areas are provided. If you are cooking on your vehicle, you have to be more selective because all the items listed above are difficult to fit onto most food trucks.

Finding a Commercial Kitchen

You'll want to rent space in a commercial kitchen that is not far from your locations or (ideally) your home. Nonetheless, finding one is not always easy, and building one is extremely costly. Unless you already own a restaurant, you will most likely be renting your kitchen space. This can be beneficial because you can meet your needs and even share the cost with other renters when ordering supplies.

"I looked online, in the Yellow Pages, and asked people I knew before finding what worked for me. Now, I share a commercial kitchen in an urban part of Seattle," explains Parfait Ice Cream truck owner Adria Shimada about starting out.

Two websites that are very helpful when searching for that elusive commercial kitchen are Commercial Kitchen For Rent at commercialkitchenforrent.com, which has a list of commercial kitchens by state, and Culinary Incubator at culinaryincubator.com, which has a map with listings of 450 kitchens that you can click on.

What You Need to Know about Commercial Kitchens

According to Tom Guiltinan, the CFO and Vice President of WHEDco, the New York–based nonprofit entity that rents three commercial kitchens from one Bronx location, "We try to be accommodating and work with clients to provide the space they need at the times they need." However, it is not always that easy. Guiltinan and other kitchen owners try hard to meet the various needs of clients. "Often businesses who come to us are still growing and aren't completely sure how much kitchen time or space they will need," says Guiltinan, who works with several mobile catering companies.

The WHEDco kitchens are kept in immaculate condition and provide counter space, convection ovens, storage areas, freezers, refrigerators, and most of what any client could possibly need, including pots and pans. "Sometimes people share a kitchen and pay less," adds Guiltinan of some of the new business clients. Clients must carry their own liability insurance with a minimum of $2 million for the aggregate coverage and $1 million for incidents. They also need to name WHEDco on the insurance coverage. "Most businesses already have this type of insurance in place," says Guiltinan.

Other Options

Schools, churches, temples, as well as local Ys may also have health inspected and certified commercial kitchens available for rent. Discuss your needs and the hours you are looking for. If you find a good match, then draw up a contract. Sometimes restaurants or catering facilities rent out space when they are not being used (which may be late night or early morning). Others have found commercial kitchen space in firehouses and hospitals. The point is—seek and you shall find. And make sure you have your agreement in writing.

Inside one of WHEDco's Commercial Kitchens in the Bronx.

Sample Listing from a Kitchen for Rent

Equipment includes: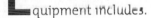

- ◯ Ten burner gas range
- ◯ Robot Coupe 'R-2 Dice' food processor with 3/8" dicer kit
- ◯ Two 40-gallon steam kettles
- ◯ 8' x 8' x 8' walk-in freezer space
- ◯ Hobart Buffalo chopper with three grater attachments.
- ◯ Electric range
- ◯ Solid door and low boy refrigerators
- ◯ 40 quart Hobart mixer

▲

What Do Customers Want?

Questions you may want to ask when looking for a commercial kitchen include:

❍ What are your hours of operations and which hours are available?

❍ What is the price? Typically a commercial kitchen will range from $125 to $350 per 10- or 12-hour day. Hourly rates can be anywhere from $10 to $40. Price also depends on the location, kitchen size, and what is included. (Some kitchens do not rent by the hour.) Long-term deals, such as for six months, will usually bring prices down. Some commercial kitchens offer unlimited access packages for $600 to $800 per month.

❍ Are utilities included?

❍ Is there an internet WiFi connection?

❍ Is all equipment included?

❍ How much time can you have at the loading dock and at what hours?

You'll also want to see if the kitchen is clean, includes working (up-to-date) equipment, and has good lighting and good ventilation. You may be asked to provide a deposit to make sure you leave the kitchen as clean as you found it.

Health and Safety First

The importance of kitchen safety cannot be overstated. In your haste to get your menu items out the door and into your kiosk or vehicle, you may find yourselves taking shortcuts. In a word, don't. Accidents and injuries slow you down and can also minimize the quality of your foods.

The simplest habit to get into is washing your hands often. Many illnesses are the result of germs traveling from dirty hands. Don't jeopardize your business. You'll also want to make sure all preparation tables, counter tops, and cutting boards are kept clean and that fruits and vegetables are washed in cold water before using.

Other tips for keeping your kitchen (whether on your vehicle or rented) safe from bacteria and accidents include:

1. Storing foods at appropriate temperatures. Make sure to check the temperatures of your refrigerator and freezers often. Cold food should be stored at 38°F or under and hot food at 165°F or above. Between 40° and 140°F is

known as the food danger zone. Food should neither be held nor consumed if it is in this temperature range.

2. Make sure all refrigerator and freezer doors close properly.

3. Keep track of food expiration dates—with a list because you are probably dealing with a lot of foods.

4. Cook foods at a minimum internal temperature and maintain that temperature for at least 15 seconds. This helps kill bacteria.

5. Be particularly careful not to undercook food.

6. Adhere to local health codes and go one step beyond. Don't wait for health department inspections to make changes. Do your own inspections. Remember, your reputation is on the line.

7. Check in periodically on the Department of Health website to see if recalls are listed for your area or if there are any new regulations.

8. Check all incoming food shipments carefully. Do not accept anything if it does not appear to be fresh. Also look for damaged cans or boxes.

9. Make sure all food equipment as well as utensils are clean and working properly.

10. Use knives and professional cutlery carefully, which means cutting away from the body and using cutting boards. And if a knife falls, don't try to catch it. Just step back and let it fall—then clean it. Also, never leave knives lying around. Put them away where they belong so nobody working in your kitchen gets injured.

11. Always have potholders and oven mitts handy—and use them. Don't improvise.

12. Have a fire extinguisher handy and make sure you and your employees know how to use it.

13. If you have employees, make sure they know how to properly use all equipment, and if necessary, post instructions.

14. If you are in a commercial kitchen, instructions are typically posted. If not, ask the kitchen manager how something works if you are unsure.

> **warning** ⚠
>
> Whether you are in a commercial kitchen or are allowed to cook in a mobile kitchen, it is very important that you wear clothing that will not get in your way or get caught in machinery. Tuck in shirts, make sure apron strings are tied, and wear comfortable non-slippery shoes with rubber soles, never high heels.

> **warning** ⚠
>
> It was funny when Monica on the TV sitcom *Friends* lost her earring in the quiche before serving it. It's not so funny when it happens for real. Put all jewelry aside when working in the kitchen or on your vehicle, or simply leave it at home.

Become Dedicated to Cleaning

You want to have all-purpose cleaners, towels, mops, rags, oven cleaner, cleaning brushes, disinfectants, degreasers, dishwasher detergents, and whatever else is necessary to clean anything you use to prepare or store foods—and kitchen floors, trash receptacles, aprons, etc. Some commercial kitchens provide their own cleaning materials. Use them. You, on the other hand, will be responsible for your vehicle or kiosk.

While dishwashers are nice, they don't always get the job done effectively, so you need to make sure whatever comes out of the dishwasher is cleaned to your liking. If you are in a hurry and need to reuse bowls or other items quickly, you'll need to do your own cleaning with a strong cleaning product followed by air drying—not towels.

You also need to make sure tongs and anything else you use to handle food is cleaned regularly. Also clean counters and cutting boards regularly. Don't take short cuts and don't leave things for the proverbial "later." As noted earlier, one of the knocks on mobile food venues has long been that they are not sanitary. All your hard work can and will go down the drain quickly if a customer gets food poisoning or discovers something that should not be in his food. And if a health inspector is not happy, word travels quickly. Remember, social media and reviews on Yelp can sink your business as fast as it can help you grow it. A lot is riding on your dedication to cleanliness.

Establish a Plan

If you establish a plan for cleaning everything and get your employees to follow suit, cleaning can become a simple routine. Brushing off the grill regularly should become a matter of habit that you need not think about. The same goes with wiping down the preparation tables. You will have daily cleaning, such as mopping floors, washing counter tops, and cleaning appliances such as the microwave, coffee maker, can opener, and so on. Floors should actually be cleaned very often with a grease-cutting floor cleaner so that you minimize the chances of anyone falling, including you. You will also have larger jobs that you need not do everyday but still need to do often, such as cleaning the refrigerator(s), ice machines, freezers, and ovens.

Typically the manufacturers of larger appliances have cleaning instructions. Don't throw out the manuals, and write down the websites if you need cleaning tips. Also, don't forget the hood needs to be cleaned a few times a year—by a professional cleaning service. If you are working in a commercial kitchen, this is the owner's responsibility. There will usually be a sticker indicating when the hood was last cleaned.

You'll also want to keep tabs on your cleaning products to make sure you have them all accounted for. Make a list of all cleaning products you need so you can buy them in large quantities when you go shopping or place an order.

tip

Although your dishwasher is a cleaning machine, it can get dirty, especially with all the wear and tear of steady use. To freshen a dishwasher, while you are cleaning up at the end of your day, try running it empty with some baking soda and vinegar. You should also take out food traps and utensil trays, and clean them as well.

Vehicle Presentation

If it isn't enough to spend a significant amount of time cleaning up the kitchen space that you rented (remember, as a renter, you still must clean up your area) and the inside of your vehicle or kiosk, you also need to remember the outside of your vehicle. Nobody wants to buy food from a truck covered with mud (not even from the famous Mud Truck in New York City). Things such as bird poop on the windows won't bring customers flocking to your cart or truck either. Make sure your vehicle is washed and soaped down regularly. Signs should be easily readable and counters should be sparkling. In a bustaurant, the seating area should be as inviting as in the finest restaurant.

Hiring Help

It's hard to go it alone in any business, especially one that requires you to be chef, server, cleaner, kitchen manager, accountant, driver, and more. While you can run a small cart or truck serving primarily pre-made and/or prepackaged goods on your own, if you should get more elaborate you will probably need some help. Many food truck owners and catering businesses are partnerships or team efforts from the start. Nonetheless, mobile food business owners typically bring on help as they grow or expand. Let's take a look at some of your hiring options.

Hiring a Chef

If you are considering the gourmet route for your business and are not a chef or do not have a particular knack for making some special items, you may want to bring in a chef. Unlike a chef in a restaurant, your menu will most likely be limited. You will, however, want to either discuss the types of food you are looking for or find a chef and see what he brings to the table—or to the plastic or paper plates, as the case may be. In many cases, not unlike a restaurant, the menu is built around a chef or someone with a knack for cooking/creating a certain type of food or beverage. In other cases, the menu may be built around what is already known in an established business such as Starbucks, where people will already know the brand and what to expect when the trucks come rolling up.

Typically, if you're thinking gourmet food truck, you want to network with restaurant owners and others in the culinary field. They can help you look locally for a chef or a chef's assistant who wants to move up the ranks. You can offer an up-and-comer exposure and the opportunity to create dishes without having to manage the kitchen—you can do that job because many young chefs are primarily interested in using their culinary skills and not running a kitchen. Many food trucks, however, are started not by "chefs" in the more traditional definition, but by people who love good food and have a knack for preparing it. They know what makes up a great sandwich or taco and are willing to experiment. In some cases, they create new and exciting menu items and they love sharing their own food fantasies with a crowd who appreciates fun, filling, and often fantastic flavors. Most food trucks are not about five-star chefs but about real people with a passion for food who are willing to roll up their sleeves and get a little greasy. One of your prime sources of young talent might be a local culinary school. Another option is to advertise on the internet or look at resumes posted at places like the American Culinary Federation, which links to the American Academy of Chefs at www.acfchefs.org. You can also check out www.ihirechefs.com.

In some cases, you may simply find someone who is a not a professional chef but is excellent at making a few items. See if she wants to turn her hobby into a career. The Mmmpanadas truck in Texas got started simply because Cody Fields and his wife Kristen, both of whom loved to cook, made damn good empanadas.

Finding Good Help

Yes, another part of your job as a business owner is hiring the help you need. Whether it's a driver, servers for your food, kitchen help, or all of the above, you will need to bring people in to work for you. First, you'll want to know what the going rate is in your part of the country. Typically, you'll find rates in the $8 to $12 an hour category for heating and serving food or helping in the kitchen.

Any person who owns and operates a small business won't hesitate to tell you that one of the most challenging aspects of being a business owner is hiring and retaining good employees. The process of hiring can be daunting if you've never done it before. Most of the labor pool available to help heat up and serve food at your kiosk or in your truck are people looking for temporary jobs while in college or until the latest recession ends. Unless someone is hoping to go into the mobile food or catering business, he or she is unlikely to be with you for years to come.

It is important to keep in mind that the people serving your customers are the frontline representatives of your business. If they are sloppy, rude, or don't do the job right, you can lose customers. With that in mind, you need to look for people who will do a good job. You want people who will:

- Be on time
- Be neat and clean
- Follow the rules and protocol that you have established
- Be courteous to customers
- Give you reasonable notice if they cannot work a shift
- Take the job seriously

Finding Applicants

Word of mouth, posting ads on local job websites and the local Craigslist, or even postings on bulletin boards in your area will generally attract applicants. Keep your postings brief. People are more apt to respond to a few lines than a dissertation. Look for people whom you think might last a while. For example, a college student in her

Don't Judge a Cook by His (or Her) Cover

It should go without saying that you want employees who are well groomed. Because employees' appearance is a reflection on the capability of your staff and the quality of your services (and because food is involved), their appearance should be neat and professional. As for trendy body wear like multiple piercing and tattoos, if you eliminate any young person who expresses him/herself that way, you may not have many candidates to choose from. As long as such personal expressions of individuality do not detract from the person's ability to make and serve food or help you in the kitchen, you should consider them as prospects.

freshman or sophomore year is more likely to stick around longer than a college senior.

If prospective employees are at least 18 (and can prove it) and are interested in a job, take their names and arrange an interview right away. Because you probably do not have a formal office, either meet at your kitchen (if you have one) or pick a neutral location, such as a Starbucks, and sit down to talk. Don't meet people at your home. Today, you also need to see the individual's Social Security Card or Passport.

Even though 16-year-olds may work legally in some parts of the country, you may find that some are not as responsible or mature as you would like. Of course it depends on the individual. Employees who are under 18 typically need to have working papers. Ask to see them.

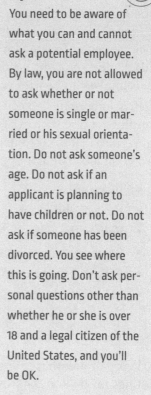

tip

You need to be aware of what you can and cannot ask a potential employee. By law, you are not allowed to ask whether or not someone is single or married or his sexual orientation. Do not ask someone's age. Do not ask if an applicant is planning to have children or not. Do not ask if someone has been divorced. You see where this is going. Don't ask personal questions other than whether he or she is over 18 and a legal citizen of the United States, and you'll be OK.

Interviews

Just as job candidates need to prepare before going on job interviews, you also need to be prepared before conducting interviews. To make your life easier, you might print up some simple/brief job application forms, in which you can ask for basic information, such as name, address, home phone and cell phone numbers, as well as job history and education. You can purchase blank application forms at office supply stores; a package of 100 usually runs about $10. If you create your own forms, keep them simple and straightforward, seeking only relevant information. You can get yourself into trouble by asking personal information, so don't do it.

When interviewing someone, don't fire questions; instead try to create a relaxed atmosphere in which each candidate can explain why she or he would be a good choice for you. Because many young candidates will not have much experience, you are better off asking about their skills and previous experience in general. Then there are the references. They are important, and you should check out at least two references. You want to get a general idea of the character, reliability, and overall personality of the potential employee. You can also go online and do background checks. Plenty of companies now run such checks for a fee. Under the Fair Credit Reporting Act, you need to use a Consumer Reporting Agency. This is because a CRA must maintain certain standards for data protection and offer dispute resolution. Using a questionable company can put you in hot water, should they violate someone's rights of privacy.

In a world where employee theft is a rising concern for most business owners, you have the right to be concerned. Therefore, along with checking references and possibly contacting previous employers, you might want to have a 30-day trial period as a condition of continuing employment. During that time, you can evaluate a person's natural aptitude for the work, his dependability, and whether he is eating more of your inventory than he is selling.

Job Description

It is also helpful to have a prepared job description that can be given to the candidate. It should include a brief description of the work to be performed, the employee's responsibilities, and the hours. During the interview, explain the job responsibilities and your expectations. Then allow the candidate to do most of the talking. As you listen, watch body language. A confident person will sit up straight in the chair and make direct eye contact with you. Someone who is both articulate and friendly will probably be good with customers. Bilingual candidates may be a plus in certain areas, but don't rule out other good candidates. Someone who looks distracted or has an attitude that indicates that he is only meeting with you because nothing better has come along (yet) may not be your best bet. While it is tough finding work in a bad economy, you cannot let yourself hire out of pity. This is your business. If your business runs into trouble or "goes under" because of your employees, you will be feeling a lot more self pity.

It's possible that you'll make a decision whether to hire someone at the initial interview, but it's better to wait until you've checked references before formally hiring anyone. You should let the applicants know the pay rate so that if it is not enough for the individual, you can cut down on the time and effort it takes to check references.

With all the taxes you are required to pay, it's no wonder some small-business owners pay employees (or themselves) off the books instead of giving Uncle Sam his due. But don't do it. You could find yourself in federal hot water if you're not square with the IRS. Remember, the IRS caught Al Capone and threw Pete Rose and Wesley Snipes in jail. Don't mess with them. All it takes is one disgruntled customer, one jealous

tip

Carefully review all safety and health regulations that pertain to your food operation with your employees. You might even walk them through each process and then ask them if they can go through the routine a couple of times. Don't just throw them in a kitchen, behind a cart, or into a truck or bus before you are convinced they know the drill.

competitor, or even one angry ex-employee (or ex-spouse) to have your food business go stale. Don't give them ammunition—pay your taxes and run an honest business.

You're Hired

Hiring someone is always both joyful and nerve-wracking. On one hand, it means you are growing your business, while on the other hand it can mean potential headaches because you are now responsible for someone else. To ease your burden, you need to remember a few simple rules about being the boss.

1. *Listen.* Letting people know what is expected of them is easy. It's also important, however, to listen and hear employee questions, concerns, and occasional good idea.

2. *Be accessible.* Schedule short meetings with employees where you can discuss what is going on before or after a busy workday. Open up a line of communications, and you'll find that you get better results.

3. *Never abuse your power.* Yes, you are the boss and you have the right to expect employees to be alert, responsible, competent, drug-and/or-alcohol free, honest, and diligent about doing their jobs whenever they are on the clock. But

> **tip** ⓘ
>
> *Be fire safe.* To prevent fires, store towels, food packaging, oils, pressurized containers, and other combustibles away from stovetops and ovens. Keep exhaust fans and ductwork free of grease build-up and regularly inspect and test fire suppression systems.

you cannot expect nonwork favors nor should you get involved in an employee's home life or personal life.

Rules and Policies

Make sure you have all warnings and proper operating instructions posted and review the correct way of doing everything with employees. Safety is a primary concern to yourself and anyone working for you. For ideas, visit the National Restaurant Association's safety page at restaurant.org.

Put as much as you can in writing, and make sure your employees see all rules and regulations. Extend this to include policies about missing work and anything else they need to know about the job.

Also, list specific grounds for termination, such as drug or alcohol use on the premises, arriving at work under the influence of drugs or alcohol, stealing, carrying an unlicensed weapon onto the property, or any lewd, rude, or violent behavior to a customer or another employee. Also include a sexual harassment policy that spells out

Are Your Employees Happy?

Keep your employees involved in the business. Ask their opinions of menu items, listen to their ideas regarding ways to move customers along faster, and so on. Some degree of involvement in the business makes for much better employee morale. And if someone makes a mistake, you should simply explain how it needs to be done correctly. Do not criticize or ridicule the employee. They will not want to work for you, and it will show in their lack of productivity. Unhappy employees can reflect upon your business or leave you when you need them most. Remember, for most of your employees this is an interim job, so you need to keep them focused. Treat people well, and with respect and they will respond accordingly. That being said, if someone is taking advantage and cannot, or will not, do the job properly, you may need to let them go. Firing someone is not easy, nor is it pleasant for most employers. However, you have a lot at risk, especially since you have to answer to the department of health as well as be up to code in numerous areas. Let people go if they are hurting your business.

how such matters will be handled—typically by using an impartial arbitrator. False harassment claims can be as damaging as real ones.

You want to be covered in case an employee or former employee decides to sue you. In a litigious society, lawsuits are common and can seriously jeopardize your business. Have all employees read your policy statement or handbook and sign that they have read it. Keep the signed paper in a safe place. This gives you written proof that they have been informed of what is expected of them.

Taxes

No discussion of business, or hiring employees, would be complete without bringing up your obligations to good old Uncle Sam. As an employer, you will be required to withhold several different types of taxes from your employees, including income tax, FICA (aka Social Security), and Medicare. The IRS also requires you to keep detailed records about the amount withheld and when it was sent in to the IRS. You will be expected to pay on schedule.

You should have an accountant for your business who will set you up with a system for paying federal, state, and local taxes in a timely fashion and recording these tax payments properly. For more information about withholding and taxes, pick up a copy of IRS Publication 15-B, *Employer's Tax Guide to Fringe Benefits,* as well as Publication 583, *Starting a Business and Keeping Records.* You can find both on the IRS website at irs.gov or at your local IRS office.

FICA

Employers incur a tax liability for every employee. You must pay the matching portion of the FICA tax, which, as of 2015, is 6.2 percent, and the matching portion of Medicare taxes, which as of 2015 is 1.45 percent. Also, workers' compensation insurance payments are mandatory in all states except Texas. They cover employees' medical expenses and disability benefits if they're injured on the job. The amount varies by state, so contact your state labor department for guidance on how much to set aside.

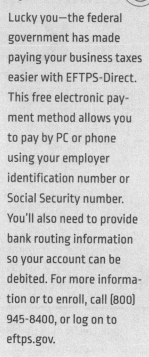

tip

Lucky you—the federal government has made paying your business taxes easier with EFTPS-Direct. This free electronic payment method allows you to pay by PC or phone using your employer identification number or Social Security number. You'll also need to provide bank routing information so your account can be debited. For more information or to enroll, call (800) 945-8400, or log on to eftps.gov.

If You Park It, They Will Come—or Not

Marketing and Promotion

Good food and service with a smile are important, but if nobody knows you are serving, you're out of luck. Marketing and promotion are key factors in the success of almost any business. While you don't necessarily need a full marketing plan, early on in your overall planning process you want to think about how you will attract customers.

▲

What's In a Name?

One of the first steps is to choose a good name, one that will draw attention. Many cart vendors, especially in Manhattan, have long been known simply by their location. People will comment on the great hot dogs from the guy on 57th Street and Fifth Avenue or 23rd and Park, but with so much competition today, it is advantageous to have a memorable name for your business.

There are plenty of clever names on the sides of food trucks, trailers, carts, and buses. Some business owners, such as Scott Baitinger and Steve Mai of Streetza pizza, had the fans name the truck, which enhanced their fan connection. Others held local contests. Some are extensions of established businesses, typically a restaurant. Still others came from crowdsourcing websites where people submitted names and the person with the best name gets paid for her idea. Most, however were the result of some brainstorming with family and clever friends. Sometimes, you'll get an idea from someone you least expected. On the television sitcom *Roseanne*, in the pre-food truck craze, when the Conners were opening a small diner from which to serve lunch, Dan and Roseanne asked their 9-year-old son D.J. what name he would use. He replied "The Lunch Box," and lo and behold it stuck and became the name of their business. So, ask around.

Some truck owners used word play like the Taste No Evil Muffins truck in Austin. You could always try a twist on a known name, such as the India Jones Chow Truck in

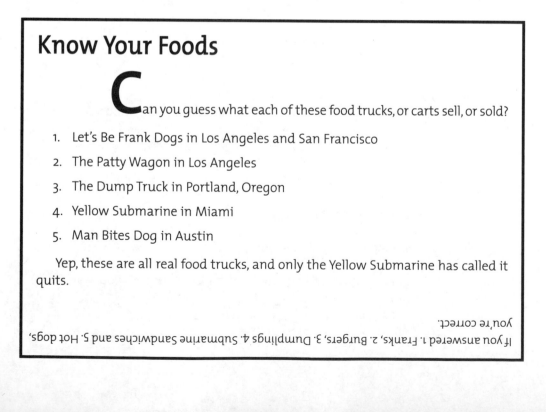

Know Your Foods

Can you guess what each of these food trucks, or carts sell, or sold?

1. Let's Be Frank Dogs in Los Angeles and San Francisco
2. The Patty Wagon in Los Angeles
3. The Dump Truck in Portland, Oregon
4. Yellow Submarine in Miami
5. Man Bites Dog in Austin

Yep, these are all real food trucks, and only the Yellow Submarine has called it quits.

If you answered 1. Franks, 2. Burgers, 3. Dumplings 4. Submarine Sandwiches and 5. Hot dogs, you're correct.

Los Angeles, or the Chairman Bao truck in San Francisco, which was later changed to the Chairman Truck.

Typically, you want your name to express what you sell in a clever manner. The Cupcake Truck in New Haven or the Cupcake Stop in New York City may not be as clever, but they get the point across and generate a lot of business. The Big Ass Sandwiches in Portland gets the point across with emphasis!

The point is, let your foods and/or ethnic menu and your location lead the way. Consider the following names to get your creative juices going:

- Only Burger in Durham (NC)
- The Sausage Guy in Boston
- Red Hook Lobster Pound in Washington, DC
- Cookie Wag in San Francisco
- Whiffies Fried Pie Cart in Portland (OR)
- Cousins Maine Lobster Truck in Phoenix and Los Angeles
- Cutie Pie Wagon in Austin (TX)
- Kooper's Chowhound Burger Wagon in Baltimore
- Bernie's Burger Bus in Houston
- Crepes Bonaparte in Los Angeles

Or consider the following ethnic names:

- The Texas Cuban in Austin (TX)
- Seoul Sausage in Los Angeles
- JAPADOG in Vancouver (Japanese-style hot dogs)
- Tamale Tracker in Chicago
- Fishlips Sushi Truck in Los Angeles

You can always simply include the meal you serve, such as the Brunch Box in Portland or the Dessert Truck in New York. You can also include your vehicle in the name, like the Magic Curry Kart in San Francisco. You can always create a catchy rhyme as Icycle Bicycle or the Shrimp Pimp did in Los Angeles. Of course rhyming a food with the word "kiosk" is virtually impossible. There has also been a trend that leans toward the "in your face" names such as the Shut Up and Eat truck in Portland or Baby's Badass Burgers in Los Angeles.

Searching for Business Names

Make sure to do a business name search before registering. You do this for three reasons:

1. It ensures that no one else in your local area is using the name
2. It makes your local authorities happy. This way, they can keep tabs on you for tax or other licensing purposes, and you go on public record in case anyone needs to look up the name of your company and find the name of the owner.
3. Most banks won't allow you to open a business checking account unless you can show them that you have registered your business name.

> **tip** (i)
>
> Keep names short and easy to remember, especially for those looking for you on a social media platform. Also, avoid generic names like Fred's Food Truck. Unless Fred is famous, it doesn't stand out or tell you what foods are featured.

See if your county clerk's office already has your chosen name on the books. Have a few variations ready in case one or two names are already taken. If your name is specific to your product, your own name, or the name of your city, such as Boston Bob's Bacon and Beans, the less likely someone else has claimed it. Typically, whether a business owner has a website or not, the company name will come up if you do a Google search, so you might try that before doing an official search at the county clerk's office. You can also contact the local chamber of commerce or simply look in the local Yellow Pages. If a name has a trademark, you can search the United States Patent and Trademark Office at uspto. gov or 1-800-786-9199 (toll free). You can also check the Thomas Register, which is part of Thomasnet.com, for registered and unregistered trademark names. It's a cross-industry database that includes hundreds of thousands of trademarks and service marks. Network Solutions is another place to look for business names online (networksolutions.com).

Registering Your Business Name

You can register your business name locally and also obtain a trademark if you choose to register your brand. First, you will do a trademark search by going to the free trademark database on the USPTO's website. Go to the USPTO's Trademark Electronic Business Center (uspto.gov) and choose "search" under the trademark section. Then follow the instructions on the screen. You'll also get all the information on how to obtain a U.S. trademark or service mark. It's not necessary for a small local business, but as your business grows, you might want to expand and sell your brand (your foods) in retail outlets. Get more information at the U.S. Trademark and Patent Office at uspto.gov.

Vehicle Design

The Dim and Den Sum truck in Cleveland was considered to have one of the more noteworthy food truck designs with a bright red octopus over bright yellow and orange stripes. Keeping an Asian-inspired theme, the truck was designed by an anonymous graffiti artist in Cleveland. While no longer on the roads, the design was particularly noteworthy when the truck was stolen in 2012 and the owners alerted their Twitter followers, one of whom recognized the unique truck design outside of his house and called the police to zero in on the stolen food truck.

The Philadelphia skyline aboard the Sugar Philly Truck is a great example of an inspiring and eye catching design. You also want to be attention grabbing like the bright red Mmmpanadas truck in Austin, Texas. Bright colors, bold lettering, and/or artwork are part of the latest in popular mobile food vehicles. Think big, bold, and exciting.

The Concept

The Louisiana Territory truck in San Jose is built around the concept of serving Louisiana-style foods, including Shrimp and Sausage Creole over rice and Louisiana Smoked Sausage. The Grilled Cheese Truck in Los Angeles is big and yellow, with a yellow menu featuring the signature Cheesy Mac a macaroni and cheese with sharp cheddar which can come fully loaded with BBQ pork and caramelized onions. Meanwhile, Van Leeuwen Artisan Ice Cream in New York City is designed to be an old-fashioned ice cream parlor on wheels with freshly made ice cream and classic sundaes.

The days of the basic food cart or truck have given way to a new brand of vehicles with concepts, or themes, that carry through from exterior design to logos, menus, and of course the foods. Your concept should be a means of distinguishing you from your competition and building your niche market. You might even name some of your foods in line with your theme. Be clever and consistent (never confusing), and you can broaden your appeal and even draw media attention.

Vehicle Wraps

You can opt for a specially designed vinyl wrap that fits around your mobile business or kiosk. Food vehicle wraps are a marvelous and cost-effective means of advertising because they look professional and are on your vehicle 24/7, generating the attention of potential customers. Advertising Vehicles (advertisingvehicles.com) is one of a number of businesses in the vehicle wrap business. Cliff Digital (cliffdigital.com) and Custom Vehicle Wraps (customvehiclewraps.com) are two of many design companies that now have a section for vehicle wraps on their websites as does San Diego vehicle wraps (sandiegovehiclewraps.com). You can find many more companies online.

Food cart and truck designers are enjoying the growth of the business while turning out some first-rate designs. Vehicle or kiosk designers are typically found on the web or through word of mouth. Food Cart USA (foodcartusa.com), All Star Carts and Kiosks (allstarcarts.com), and Cart-King (cart-king.com) design first-rate mobile food vehicles both inside and out. They also walk you through other steps, such as making sure their interior design will meet your local health and safety codes. Road Stoves (Roadstoves.com) sells both new and used trucks, rents them as well and also does advertising and promotion, consulting, provides digital applications, and organizes events where food trucks can sell their goodies.

Your Logo

A logo can set your vehicle apart from the competition. It is a distinguishing graphic representation of your business and its value. You can use the trademark symbol TM to indicate that it is your logo, even if it is not yet an official trademark.

Look for local designers and artists to come up with logos and graphics for your business. Sometimes you'll find great talent just waiting to be discovered in local art classes or art schools. Ask around. Because your truck will be unique onto itself, other cart or truck owners may recommend artists or designers. Save yourself and the artist or designer some time by looking at some of his previous works before asking him to do something for you.

Menu Design

Design your menu to fit the style and theme of your truck. Selling cupcakes? Post the menu on the cart in the shape of a cupcake. You'll want a menu that is appropriate with your brand and style, so use your color scheme and design. Read as many menus as you can find from your competitors. Get an idea of what styles and layouts you like.

Some menus simply list the offerings with prices while others include some detail about the menu items. For example, here's how Adria in the Parfait Ice Cream truck describes her flavors:

Butter Toffee Crunch

We make our own butter toffee, coated with dark chocolate and hazelnuts, and then add generous chunks of this delicious confection to our vanilla bean ice cream. The result is a better tasting version of "Heath Bar Crunch" without any of the artificial or hydrogenated ingredients in industrially manufactured candy.

Such descriptions can enhance your brand by letting customers know that your foods are all-natural or from a interesting locations. Have various versions of menus for various locations—for example, your website menu can include more detail than the small posted menu or a sandwich board. Consider where your menus will be posted, such as on your:

- Vehicle
- Website
- Printed materials
- Sandwich boards (perhaps)

Design accordingly so that your foods and prices are easily readable for those in a hurry.

tip

For comprehensive up-to-date information about truck designs, marketing, menus, health codes, or practically anything else going on in the mobile food truck industry, check out Mobile Food News (mobilefoodnews.com).

Social Media

Part of the reason for the surging popularity of food trucks is social media. Twitter, Foursquare, Facebook and Instagram are the hottest marketing tools for mobile food entrepreneurs to stay in touch with their customers, fans and followers.

Social media literally lets foodies follow their trucks to new location. But you have to know what you're doing to make the most out of these new tools. First, you need to know the medium since platforms like Facebook, Twitter, Instagram, Foursquare, and others have their own culture and demographics. The limited number of characters makes Twitter the place for fast information and rapid flowing conversations. You need to take some time to engage with your followers while tweeting your latest location and news (specials, new menu items, an upcoming event, etc.) regularly. Facebook is conversational but you can check in and change your postings, photos, etc., at more scheduled times. Both of these platforms require some familiarity and a concerted effort to stay fresh with daily postings. Someone on your team should be the social media person, which helps maintain a sense of consistency with your posts.

Know your demographics and the demographics of the platform. Facebook will reach the most people, Twitter is the fasted way to spread news quickly and Instagram is a visual site which is a terrific way to display your food, your truck, your crew, or anything that will grab the user visually. Foursquare is a location finder, so you can simply make sure people always know where to find you.

It's advantageous to get an idea of what other successful truck owners have been doing on social media over the past few years. You can learn from those who have been there and done that. See how far in advance they post upcoming events and what posts get the best responses.

You also want to pay attention to the responses you are getting, not only on social media but at review sites like Yelp, which is also an important site for food truck owners. What do people like/dislike about what you are doing? What postings are generating likes? What menu items are getting the best responses? The best reviews? You can learn a lot from your followers and customers. You can also interact to some extent without reaching out to everyone and without arguing or debating with your fans, followers, or critics. Keep in mind that just as quickly as social media can help you, if you take a negative turn if you get into arguments or anger your followers. And, if something goes wrong and makes its way onto social media, such as a situation where you were unable to show up at an event that you were scheduled to attend, be forthright, apologetic, and even offer a discount in that area. In short, be ready to put out fires and make amends when necessary.

Websites and Phone Apps

When searching for a food truck in a busy city, there are websites and apps that can help customers find the kind of mobile foods that they are looking for. One website, FoodTrucksIn.com, also creating an app, provides details on where you will find over 4,200 food trucks, carts, trailers, and stands in nearly 900 cities. Adding roughly 40 trucks a day and updating listings every 90 days FoodTrucksIn.com is growing rapidly while staying abreast of changes in the industry for both customers and truck owners.

Along with helping people follow their favorite trucks, "we are finding strong ways to attract new customers and becoming a national resource connecting people with mobile food wherever they travel," explains Eric Weiner, the owner of FoodTrucksIn.com. "We can also find catering trucks for parties or for bands, for after their event," says Weiner who is also helping truck, cart, and trailer owners by listing vendors in areas they serve. "Whether it's truck maintenance or a nearby place to buy fresh food or ingredients, we want to be able to help owners locate vendors," adds Weiner of the multifaceted site and upcoming app. Among the other popular food truck sites/apps, you'll find Roaming Hunger, which provides locations of the trucks, menu information, hours or operation, and more.

As a truck owner, you can be set up with Roaming Hunger, where information and location can be updated regularly. Your profile page can also provide fans with all they need to know about your truck.

Another app on which you want to be listed is TruckSpotting as well as the Truckspotting.com website. Along with allowing foodies to find your location through your GPS, you can also post your profile, menu, food prices, upcoming events, and so forth. TruckSpotting is also a free downloadable iPhone or Android app, which provides hungry customers with the location of trucks in the city that they are visiting.

tip ⓘ

Los Angeles has been a forerunner in the food truck revolution. The iPhone application "LA Street Food" has become popular in the area. Look for similar apps for other major cities.

Your Website

For a truck or even a cart owner, a website is essential, even if you are using Facebook, Twitter, and various mobile applications. Plain and simple, people still use the web to find out about a business. Your website is another tool in your marketing plan.

Designing Your Website

A new business owner should look at the sites of similar businesses to get an idea of the look that he wants for the website. While you cannot take someone else's content, you can get the general idea of the layout and even the colors you want.

Typically your website will contain the following:

- *Homepage.* Photos of the food, photos of the truck, easy links to the other pages on your site (such as your About Us pages), your Twitter thread, and the most relevant current news is typically found on the homepage. Like the rest of the site, the homepage should take on the colors and concept of your vehicle or kiosk. You should also include a link to your Facebook page and anywhere else you can be located. You might have your menu on the homepage; if not, it should be a click away.

- *About Us.* Tell your story in a brief and clever way. Read other About Us pages to get an idea of what to say and then in your own words tell the story of how you got started and why. People don't need your life story so edit, edit, edit.

- *Menu.* Display your menu on a colorful, eye-catching page in conjunction with your colors. Make sure to update foods and prices as they change.

- *Gallery.* Some recent pictures of the foods, the truck, customers (with their signed consent), and even you as the owner(s) can be posted. Update if you attended a recent event or have something new to show.

- *Press.* Newspapers and magazines are clamoring to write about the latest in mobile foods—as soon as you get coverage, post it on your website.

- *Map and/or Schedule.* If you know where you're going to be in the next week or next month, post a schedule and/or map.

tip

Don't forget your website is up there day after day. Update it often. Keep it current. Provide fresh content such as upcoming events where fans and followers can find you. Be informative and entertaining. Give people a reason to keep coming back.

- *Contact Page.* Make sure people can reach you easily.

tip ⓘ

Link to other sites and have them link to you. The Mmmpanadas website (mmmpanadas.com), for example, links to grocery stores in and around Austin that also carry their empanadas. Most often, sites you link to will reciprocate.

For a catering company handling parties and other outings, you'll want to have a little more detail on your website because clients can hire you or at least inquire directly about such services from your site.

Your website should immediately convey what you can offer clients and why you should be their choice to hire. This can be done through photos of parties and celebrations you have catered, along with photos of food and even a few themes. (Get permission from clients to use photos from their events.) Also on your site should be your business name and logo, easily accessible contact information, and details on what kinds of catering you do with sample themes and menus. You may want to include a few short testimonials. Keep them brief because nobody wants to read an endless review. Also, try to maximize your responses by offering online deals, such as 10 percent off if you respond via email. Your goal is to start a dialogue about what catering needs a client may have and how you can fulfill them.

Once people respond to your website, make a smooth and early transition from emails to a phone call and even an in-person meeting to show them what you can do for them. Of course, you also need to make it clear, on the website, exactly where you do business. If you're based in Ann Arbor, Michigan, for example, someone from Boise, Idaho, probably won't be in your catering area. Don't quote prices on your website, although you can give a range. Typically you'll use a per person rate on a tiered level. Also provide options and offer lower prices for more people. More on pricing later.

Web Layout and Design

It's important to put the most important data and great photos high up on the pages so that people need not scroll down and down. You can keep older information farther down, such as an event you attended a month ago, but keep recent and important news up high on the page(s). Also make sure your colors and graphics look good not only on your computer screen but also on various mobile devices because more and more people are using their phones and tablets than their laptops. Don't waste time on fancy graphics that may take too long to load. Nobody has time to wait.

If you look for a local web designer in your area, make sure to show her other sites that you like, and be sure that she develops a site that is user-friendly and easy to maneuver. It's your business, so get what you want. For your purposes, the site does not need to have sales capabilities unless you are selling promotional items like T-shirts, mugs or cups, caps, key chains, bottle openers, or something that exemplifies your truck or cuisine.

From a technical standpoint, it is important that all pages link easily to the information the individual is seeking. Don't make visitors to your website jump hurdles to find what they are looking for or they will give up. Check links often to make sure they are still working.

Some excellent websites to check out are parfait icecream.com, gofishtruck.com, and samschowder mobile.com.

warning

Look carefully at the other sites a web designer has done in the past. If they all appear to have a similar style and it's not what you want, do not assume for a second that this person can deviate from the norm just for you. Habits are hard to break. You need someone who sees your vision, not a variation of her own.

Establishing an Online Presence

As many business owners have learned over the past decade, just because you have a website doesn't mean people will find it. Even if you optimize your site with key words, links, and other tricks of the trade, that still doesn't assure you that people will flock to it.

You need to maintain a presence on Twitter and have your website, Facebook page, and Instagram pages linked and clearly printed on your menus and included in any media interviews you do. Linking with other retailers and getting your listing in all local online directories also draws attention to your website. Good content about food and topics your audience can munch on is also important in building a following and increasing hits. Blogging is very popular, but you need to make your blog interesting and fun to read. Also, drawing in new business by adding tidbits of clever information, trivia, e-cards, jokes, or anything else relating to your food or your overall theme is beneficial. Then spread the word, share with friends or fans, re-tweet comments on Twitter, or, if you post a video on YouTube, make sure to share it. Be creative and generate a buzz. This way your followers can help promote your business.

Marketing and Promotional Ideas

Once upon a time a food truck or food cart might have been located nearby a new store in hopes of trying to capture the crowd as they left the grand opening. Today, a

▲

food truck is often a co-star, or in some cases a main attraction. Ever since the *Great Food Truck Race* first aired on the Food Network in August 2010, many trucks and carts have taken on personalities of their own. The show, which has continued to generate strong ratings, has proven inspiring for soon-to-be truck owners. Despite a little TV glamour and reality show rivalry, the program provides a glimpse at some of the hard work that goes into running a food truck. The owners of the 2014 winning truck, the Middle Feast Truck in Los Angeles, exemplify the hard work that comes with the territory.

Giveaways

One of the most tried and true means of building a following is by giving something away, whether it's a promotional item or a sample of your product, which in this case means food. Providing it fits into your marketing budget, consider giveaways as a standard means of generating a crowd. Food companies have been doing this for years by providing free samples in supermarkets.

Contests

You can promote a simple contest through social media as well as from your vehicle. You might, for example, look for someone to name your latest culinary extravaganza (aka your latest food creation). Prizes need not be spectacular, just enough to convince fans to participate. Make a big deal about the drawing of the winner so that people will be on hand and buying your food!

Word-of-Mouth Marketing

Just give 'em something to talk about. The cheapest means of spreading the word is by having others do it for you, which is also a form of viral marketing. There are many ways in which you can set up a "Tell a Friend" 15 percent discount. You could also have singing and dancing servers might get you noticed, or perhaps you can have someone dressed up as a mascot to hand out balloons and coupons near your location.

Attending or Staging Local Events

Find out about local events well in advance by looking at local listings and even last year's listing since many local events are annual. If you believe the turnout will make it worth your while, plan to attend, which usually means reserving a space and possibly leaving a deposit. As Eric Weiner of FoodTrucksIn.com points out, many popular food trucks reach a point in which they are asked to come to events to draw their crowd. You can also do what some food truck owners have done and stage anything from a party to a puppet show for kids (if you sell ice cream or kid favorites). Be creative. Also, have all licenses and permits in hand before staging such an event. Local ordinances will let you know when, where, and how long you can stage a public event—plan well in advance. Check with the county clerk or other local municipalities.

Advertising and Sponsorships

Advertising generates attention for the sponsor and income for the food truck owners. You can sell advertising or even trade with other businesses. Put their ads on your menu and your ad in their storefront or on their menu. Bartering for ad space is a great deal because you have mobile visibility and/or distribution. It's also a plus because paying for advertising can become costly very quickly.

From a sponsorship standpoint, you can be a sponsor of a local event such as a local race for a local charity. This shows your business off while you help a worthy cause. A business running an event could also bring you in as an added attraction. For example, ABC Family, while launching its summer TV lineup, hired a food truck to give out free cupcakes. This brought the food truck to the attention of a new audience of cupcake lovers. And, when *Game of Thrones* was just about to make its first splash on HBO, New York and Los Angeles were home to Game of Thrones food trucks with five menu items representing the five regions of Westeros. While these trucks were run by HBO, imagine landing a sponsor of a television show, movie, or video game on the side of your truck. Think big bucks!

Let other business owners know that you can be bought or even be asked to show up if it looks like there will be a good turnout. Also, look to become a part of your community. Sponsor a youth sports team or turn up at a blood drive. The more visibility you have locally, the more you build your reputation.

Customer Relations: Service with a Smile

One of the simplest ways of drawing repeat customers doesn't involve technology nor does it require you to dip into your budget. It is simply by having good customer relation skills. This begins with a smile, a polite thank-you, and paying attention to the needs of your customers. Courtesy has become a dying art. Don't let your truck be part of this demise. Train your employees to be accommodating, polite, and courteous at all times. If there is a problem, make sure they are ready and willing to do what is necessary to solve it to the customer's satisfaction. Remember, your reputation is on the line, and with the immediacy of social media, the last thing you need is someone badmouthing your business.

Public Relations

No, you don't want to spend thousands of dollars a month on a public relations firm when you can spread the word yourself through social media and by word of mouth. You do, however, want to get into the mass media if at all possible. Generating stories about your business, whether in a blog or a televised news report, can draw customers and will cost you next to nothing.

Because more and more writers and reporters are now covering the mobile food industry and food trucks and/or carts have been featured in all sorts of major publications, it's not all that hard to get coverage. In fact, many food truck websites now feature a page of press clippings.

From a kiosk to a bustaurant, you can generate attention through:

- New and innovative menu items
- The concept and design of your kiosk or vehicle
- Special promotional activities or events
- Partnering with a major store or well-known business
- Expanding with additional vehicles or kiosks
- Media exposure through interviews
- Celebrity visitors, even a local celebrity can to the trick

Of course good food and good service is a big plus when trying to generate media attention.

For your part, you need to contact any and all local publications as well as websites that follow the mobile food industry or write about the latest trends. You can tweet a local reporter or blogger, or for longer news items, email a one-page press release. Make sure to keep your information concise, stick to the point, and lead with the most exciting and eye-catching aspect of your news. Focus on news that might be of interest to your following. You can hire a local freelance PR writer for help or look online for press release writing tips. Also do what Mmmpanadas does, and link you're articles and media mentions to a page on your website.

tip

Get a feel for which websites your customers visit and which magazines or local newspapers they read. Get the name of the editor and/or web content manager, and tweet or email that person. It's very important to reach the right individuals. Also, take note of writers and reporters who have written about mobile food previously and save their information. Don't send them every little bit of information. Wait until you have something interesting, enticing, or mouth watering to report.

Mobile Event Catering

While mobile catering is sometimes used to sum up all types of mobile food vehicles, in this book mobile catering is defined as those businesses that cater specific events in various places. Much of what has been discussed thus far—such as menu options, licenses, hiring employees, startup costs, and finding a commercial kitchen—apply to

▲

mobile catering trucks. However, there are some key differences that are discussed in this chapter.

Catering Business Fundamentals

To run an effective catering business, you need to start by figuring out what type of catering best suits you. It's hard to be everything to every potential client, especially when starting out. As your business grows, you can take on more challenges, larger parties, and more adventurous themes. To begin, however, you should start with some manageable ideas. Perhaps you have a few themes that you do well that would be great for cocktail parties or kids parties.

You can offer to cater events much in the manner that a food truck works a festival, by parking and serving—only in your case you are strictly for hire and not selling individual items. If permitted in your jurisdiction, you can cook on your vehicle and for private parties even sell alcohol—know the rules in advance. Don't listen to rumor or your client who may want you to sell beer or wine because they say so. Have a copy of the local ordinances available. Most mobile caterers use a commercial kitchen and transport food to parties and/or local events. Unlike a food truck or cart making a daily run, however, you may not have a set schedule when starting out. You will probably have occasional bookings—three one week and perhaps none the next—so you need to discuss flexible scheduling with the kitchen representative. Unfortunately, using a commercial kitchen on such a scattered basis typically costs you a little more than having a set long-term deal. Look for a kitchen that can provide such flexibility and work with you as you grow.

Know Your Market

Before you can cater to a niche market, you need to know what is popular at such occasions in your city, county, or region. What foods are being served at:

- Nonprofit groups and associations
- Corporate lunches and parties
- Kids parties
- Special celebrations/parties (graduations, retirement parties, Bar/Bat Mitzvahs)
- Charitable events
- Red-carpet opening nights or other grand openings
- Launch parties for new businesses

- Engagement parties and weddings
- Communities events, picnics, parties, and celebrations

While you may not be the next Tareq and Michaele Salahi (the infamous White House party crashers), you can still scout all sorts of gatherings. If you can't finagle an invitation, then ask people you know to take notes on each of the catered events they attend. Scout your competition to see what they've cooked up. Take note of whether any parties have made the local food pages, gossip columns, or websites. Play detective, and figure out menu options for each of the demographic groups. Remember, you can't please every group—yet. Keep in mind that weddings are probably the most challenging events to cater because so much is riding on them and you need to have a very solid reputation.

Corporate events and kids' parties will obviously want different menu items. But what does the red-carpet crowd eat in your area? What are popular snacks for retirement parties? What does the late night chic crowd eat? Again, know what you can make and make well. Then determine which groups are best for you to approach.

Setting Up Your Menu

Of course you need to decide on your menu items. They will be built around what you (or your chef) know how to make, the size of the parties you feel comfortable catering, and the types of parties you are planning to cater.

After researching your potential market, you need to consider what menu best suits your needs. Remember to factor in the availability of foods in your area, how much help you will have preparing food, and the time element from booking a client to the actual event. It's advantageous to set a deadline for changes, such as three days in advance or even a week for larger parties. After that clients cannot change menu items or the number of guests without an additional fee. The more you can plan ahead, the better off you will be. To play it safe, you can have some last-minute options always at the ready, such as pastas, salads, and other items that won't cost you much to have on hand.

tip

The USDA has a standard for nutritious eating. It follows what is called the Food Pyramid. This pyramid consists of recommended percentages of grains, vegetables, fruits, dairy products, and meat and beans for a healthy diet. When making up your menu, consider these five important categories, especially in a health-conscious environment.

▲

Catering Themes

Start with one or two themes and plan menus accordingly. Later on you can always expand the list if business is going well. Popular themes include:

○ Comfort foods

○ Outdoor BBQs

○ Clam bakes or picnics for groups or associations

○ Ethnic dining (Mexican Fiesta, A Taste of Italy, New Orleans, etc.)

Your menu is also predicated on the cost of foods. The more you spend, the more you need to charge. With that in mind, you should look at a markup of three times your expenses. So if a specific dish costs you $7 to buy and prepare per serving, you would need to charge $21 per person for that menu item. Have a variety of menu choices at different price points. People like variety. Lunches can be hot or cold, pastas, meats, fish, salads, sandwiches, quiche, etc., while the main course for a dinner is typically a choice of fish, poultry, or meat, plus a vegetarian offering. Of course this can vary depending on your theme or demographic group. For kids' parties, you might opt to go with hot dogs, chicken fingers, or fish sticks, which is a variation on meat, chicken, or fish, plus pasta as a vegetarian choice. Also offer various ways of preparing dishes, such as grilled, roasted, poached, or fried. And remember to cater to people with various food preferences, such as vegan or kosher, as well as those individuals with food allergies. Be prepared. Try to avoid offering to customize a menu for a client. It's better to stick with what you know than promising them anything custom. Trying something new may be cost ineffective, and even worse, it may not turn out very well unless someone on your staff knows how to make it.

Marketing Ideas

Because you have no brick-and-mortar storefront and are not driving around, unless you are headed to/from an event, you need to do more marketing than restaurants or mobile food vendors.

You want to get your name to as many event planners as possible, and if you go the wedding route, you'll want to become known to wedding planners as well. Some marketing ideas include:

- Using the social network to talk about your themes and your menu choices
- Starting a blog on recipes and food
- Spreading the word among friends, family members, and neighbors, as well as local organizations and associations
- Making sure to have business cards to hand out everywhere
- Having a brochure with photos of your foods and a list of themes included—and hand them out often
- Building your website and maintaining it with interesting content

Unlike the mobile food trucks and carts, your location is not important on your website. Instead you want to feature your upcoming availability, your menu, and your themes. Of course you also need to make sure clients know how they can reach you. It is also a good idea to promote upcoming themes in advance. For example, start hyping your seasonal holiday party themes at least six months ahead of time. Note. It can be advantageous to check out the website of the National Association of Catering Executives (nace.net).

Of course the most important way of getting started is by serving great food at a party or luncheon and making sure people talk about it. To get the ball started, offer your services at a few small parties or luncheons at an unbeatable price—free. Yes, this will be part of your startup cost, but if you get a few jobs under your belt and generate some buzz, word of mouth can have you making back your investment in a hurry. Catering is very much a word-of-mouth business. If someone likes what you serve and how you manage the party, they will tell their friends. Also, get some positive testimonials and

tip

Along with developing several menu options (not too many) for your catering business, you should also think about seasonal favorites so that you can be ready to do the corporate Fourth of July summer barbecue as well as the corporate holiday party. Remember, return business is very important. Plan your clients' next party even before they think of it, and let them know you are ready when they are. You might even send them a tasty treat with a reminder that the holidays are coming up and holiday parties are one of your specialties.

warning

Never book a party or event until you know exactly how much you can prepare and store in your kitchen and carry on your vehicle. And we cannot emphasize enough—never do a party without a deposit in advance.

Learning to Serve

First, it's important to have a number of cater waiters and/or crew members available with flexible schedules. Unlike a truck or cart that is on the streets nearly every day, you might go two or three weeks without a catering event until you become established. Therefore, you need reliable, dependable people whom you can call when you need them. Often these are students, actors, models, or people with unusual or unsteady schedules.

Some of your staff may need a crash course on serving etiquette. There are proper ways to serve and to act when catering a party. A well-trained staff can enhance your chances of being hired for upcoming gatherings.

put them on your website. And don't forget to post photos of your delicious platters and presentations online.

Professionalism

You need to be as professional as possible when working parties. This is especially important for your staff. Matching attire is in vogue, although you may not need uniforms or black tie (unless your specialty is black tie affairs such as weddings). As least have shirts or vests with your logo on them for a professional look—and to promote your business.

You need to discuss the details of an upcoming party or event with your clients, spelling out exactly what you can offer. Know your capabilities. Sure you might have a maximum of 50 for an office party, but can you cook for 20 more and price accordingly? Flexibility is very important, as is knowing what is beyond your limits.

It's important that you are as professional as possible when meeting with prospective clients. Because you are a mobile business, you should either visit a client's office (with something tasty) or meet at a neutral location (again with something tasty—but if you meet in a Starbucks or a restaurant, minimize the goodies).

Catering Contracts

It is professional to have a contract in place for any event you are catering. Sit down with an attorney (one who is good with contracts) and spell out all the possible scenarios. Have clients sign contracts that include the where and when of the event, the foods they have selected, the quantity, and the costs. Also make sure you have a very specific arrangement when it comes to payment. A deposit is very important so you do not spend money on food and get stuck taking a loss. Typically, you do not have an inventory other than paper goods and other non-perishables so you are, therefore, shopping for food with your client's money. Also make it clear that the bill is due at the end of the event or when you deliver the food if you are not being hired to serve. Let them know acceptable means of payment. Also don't forget to attend to the what-ifs in your contract. What if it is an outside party and there is inclement weather? Do you offer a partial refund? Can you handle the move to an indoor location? Do you charge more for setting up twice? How much? What if you are catering a party for adults, but there are five young children, do you charge them less per person? Do you charge them at all? Do you have kid-friendly foods available? You should, at a lower price. Consider all of the possibilities or "what if's."

> **tip**
>
> If you are starting out small, part time, on weekends, or simply just getting your feet wet, you might only need expensive equipment and supplies a couple of days a week. In such a case, you might consider leasing some of your equipment.

From Setup to Cleanup

If you will be serving at a party, visit the location in advance (or at least get an overview of the room) before you arrive with food and any decorations. You'll want to come in ready to set up with a clear idea of the facility. If you need to supply tables and chairs, know that in advance and be ready to set up. Many catering companies do not take on that extra burden because it means a larger truck or even a separate truck.

> **warning**
>
> Something smells fishy. If hot foods will be out on the buffet for a period of time, some may start to smell. Fish is especially delicate. Opt for crab cakes or fried oysters, or sell clients on your delicious sushi.

Make sure to map out everything from setup to cleanup and know who will handle each task, especially getting rid of debris. When you leave a location, it should look exactly as it did before you arrived. If you need electrical outlets, find out where they are. Have a small, quiet portable generator just in case. Know what you need and what they require in advance so you can be as inconspicuous as possible.

Food Transport

tip ⓘ

Transport food in insulated or electrically heated/cooled food carriers in order to keep foods at a safe temperature. Remember that foods should not be kept between 40 and 140 degrees. Make sure to follow all health regulations for your state when preparing and transporting foods.

There are a lot of tricks to the trade, many of which you will learn as you go forward. In fact, most caterers have developed their own systems over time. One of the most important things to remember is that food must be ready to go at the time specified in your agreement. With this in mind, you'll want to get cold dishes, especially those that need to be cooked, out of the way and into the refrigerator in advance, so they have time to cool down before the trip. The bottom line is that some foods are better choices for catering because they travel well. Chilled or room-temperature dishes such as salads, soups, and braised foods work well, while foods that can dry out can be a problem. Know ahead of time which foods travel better than others and what you can do to keep foods fresh and moist when serving.

If you have catering trays and bowls that you can fit conveniently into your refrigerator onboard your truck or van, then you will have less food to move around when you arrive. Make sure you have enough trays, bowls, lids, covers, and wrap to cover foods you plan to transport. AirPots with handles are good for carrying coffee (check out airpot.com). Make sure you have insulated food carriers to keep food cold or warm as necessary. And before transport, make sure you have everything you need, from the foods to the napkins, toothpicks, and corkscrews. Make a transport checklist and follow it closely. Not having something on hand that you need is embarrassing.

For hot foods, make sure to have them heated and ready to go according to your schedule. Microwaves in your vehicle come in handy for some foods and burners at the party or event for others. Ask in advance if the location has a kitchen where you can heat up foods.

In many instances you will simply be asked to drop off platters and not serve. In such cases you need to have an abundance of disposable catering supplies at the ready. Here, your presentation of the foods on the tray can also score points. Good food plus a good presentation equals positive word of mouth.

Check out Food Service Warehouse at foodservicewarehouse.com for a host of disposable options. You might also visit Catering Supplies.com (cateringsupplies.com), or A S Catering Supplies, Ltd. (ascateringsupplies.com). Look for recyclable paper goods if possible.

Catering from Your Vehicle

If you are promoting your vehicle to be parked at parties or local events, such as a corporate picnic, you have home field advantage because you are working in or around the friendly confines of your truck or cart. Knowing what foods the client wants, what hours you are serving, and who is paying are the key concerns. If, for example, you are asked for 300 hot dogs, 200 burgers, and 400 cans of soda, you need to be paid accordingly for the foods plus your time.

Typically you should not be collecting money from the guests unless such terms are established in advance. Logistics is often an important issue. Campgrounds or parks require that you have a permit to park on the specific location. If you do these types of events often, check with the local parks department in advance. Parks are also very strict about where barbecues can be held. Make sure you are in accordance with the park regulations as well as those set forth by the fire department. The people planning the event should handle this, but often they do not. Don't leave it up to them, double-check and/or take matters into your own hands.

If you are asked to park on private property, make sure it is the client's property or she has written permission in advance for you to park there. Make sure you visit the site ahead of time. Stories of trucks that could not get down park roads or were too wide to make it over a small bridge are funny later on, but were not when the caterer tried to get to the party. Check out exactly where you are going and where you are parking.

Specialty Services

You can handle the food only or offer specialty services yourself or in conjunction with other vendors. Providing decorations, entertainers, or other party enhancements can bring in extra income while expanding your network. It can also be an extra headache when trying to arrange for a pony ride in a luxury-housing complex. Be careful what you promise. Of course, those same entertainers that you bring to a catered party can recommend your services to other people they know. Likewise, you can advertise on each other's brochures, fliers, and websites.

Specialty services, however, can also mean finding a special item for the birthday boy or supplying the cake from a local bakery. Sometimes this extra touch can make you the favored caterer in a community. Even bringing a gift for the guest of honor or a set of golden candleholders for the anniversary couple can be a special something that sets you apart from your competition.

The All-Important Costs

Every successful business needs to go from the red to the black by acquiring green. Yes, making money is what differentiates a business from a hobby. And while a mobile food vehicle or mobile catering business would be an expensive hobby, it is not that costly as a business. In fact, one of the reasons food-loving entrepreneurs take this route is to avoid the higher overhead of a restaurant although some may decide to go that route later on after proving themselves and building a following in the mobile food world.

Dollars and Sense

Sure, planning the menu and designing the truck are fun aspects of the business. However, culinary skills and creativity not withstanding, any food business, is just that—a business. Zach Brooks, founder and owner of Midtownlunch.com, a website which features inexpensive eateries and food trucks in New York, Los Angeles, and other cities, says it's the same as starting a restaurant, the only difference is you're on wheels and you have a low overhead. "If you're getting into this business because you think you're going to get rich or be part of the new hot trend, don't do it," says Brooks, adding that it's a lot of hard work and the payoff is not usually that great for 12 hour days. "But, if the idea of driving a truck around, serving your own foods, being a part of that street culture, and making an okay living while doing what you enjoy sounds good, then by all means do it," he adds.

While foodies are turning the Food Network chefs and some of the hottest truck owners into major stars, the majority of entrepreneurs in the industry work long and hard without getting famous or even a lot of recognition for their efforts. Some are finding themselves in newspaper or magazine articles, or in blogs, while others are growing a major fan base on Twitter. Nonetheless, the hard work remains and the bottom line is still about making money.

To succeed in the business, you need to become cost savvy. "You learn about spending and saving money as you work in the industry," says Marcus Gotay, kitchen manager of WHEDco's four commercial kitchens in New York City, three of which are rented to the public on a regular basis. "You take inventory and see where you are spending money on a weekly or monthly basis and where you can spend more or cut back."

There's no set formula, but as in any bus-iness, especially when dealing with the food possibilities, you need to know what you are spending on the product(s) you sell, whether it's a cookie, an empanada, or a steak. You don't have to pay rent like a brick-and-mortar business, but you do have vehicle maintenance, kiosk space rental, parking permits, and other costs that need to be factored into the equation.

> **warning**
>
> One fact that many food cart and truck owners need to be careful about is the cost of parking their vehicle. Looking for lower rental (yet health department approved) overnight parking can be a big plus. With charges of $200 plus per month, parking costs can eat away at profits very quickly.

Obviously if you are selling a prepackaged item, it will be much easier to keep your costs in line. But for those of you who are cooking your own food, it's a little trickier. When you add up your ingredients, packaging, marketing, logo, and all the other ongoing expenses and divide by the number of products or portions that you can sell in a given day, week, month or year, the question will be: Are you making a profit?

One former high-end cookie caterer realized, after three years of losing money, that it was costing nearly $75 per cookie to run the business. That was reason enough to shut down. On the other hand, Celine Legros, owner and chef behind Les Canelés de Céline, a French pastry mobile caterer in New York City, calculated the costs of her ingredients, commercial kitchen rental, packaging, shipping, and everything else she spent on the business to determine that she was spending only $.17 per pastry. Therefore, if she sold a pastry at three times her cost or $.50 each, she would make $.33 per pastry. Therefore 250 pastries for a catered party would cost her $42.50 to make, and she would charge $125, or perhaps $100 at a bulk discount rate. Of course, if her competitors were selling French Pastries at $89 for 250, she might have to take a slightly lower markup—or prove that hers are worthy of the higher price.

The point is, you need to look very carefully at the type(s) of foods you are making, the cost of ingredients (including the cost of traveling to get ingredients or having them shipped to you), and all other factors involved in preparing your foods so you don't end up with a $75 cookie.

Business Startup Costs

There's no set formula for determining how much it costs to start a business. The field is broad, and there are too many possibilities. Clearly, a cart will typically cost less than a truck, and a prepackaged product such as ice cream, candy, or cans of soda are typically cheaper than making your own foods or beverages.

For your purposes, you want to make a list of each of everything you need from the truck, cart, van, kiosk, bus, and retrofitted equipment to marketing and promotion costs and home office equipment. The worksheet on page 116 is for you to fill in your rough numbers.

The range of costs varies greatly. You might spend $3,000 on a food cart, $500 on your initial food bill, $400 on permits and registrations, $200 on marketing, $300 on an attorney, $500 on insurance, and $300 for the first month to park and clean the cart. Tack on $300 in other miscellaneous costs, and you're off and running for $5,500.

On the other hand, you could spend $ 90,000 on a retrofitted food truck, $1,000 on initial ingredients, $2,000 on permits and licenses, $2,000 for the first month of a

Sample Cost Worksheet

Your costs will vary according to the type of food operation, so add in other costs as they pertain to starting up your particular business.

Startup Costs

Cart purchase	$
Retrofitting (the cart may already meet your needs/specifications)	
All permits and licensing	
Cooking supplies	
Market research	
Website design	
Menu design and printing (include menu boards, handouts, etc.)	
Initial advertising and marketing	
Initial food purchase	
Initial paper and soft goods purchase	
Insurance	
Bookkeeping (ledger and/or computer program)	
Credit card processing capabilities	
Initial parking rental or deposit	
Initial commercial kitchen rental or deposit	
Accounting and legal fees	
Miscellaneous	
Total Startup Cost	$

commercial kitchen rental, $300 for the first month of parking and maintaining the truck, $1,700 on kitchen supplies, $3,000 on marketing and promotion, $2,000 on packaging, $1,000 to set up a small home office for bookkeeping, $2,000 on insurance, and $1,000 in miscellaneous costs for a grand total of $ 106,000.

Compared to a restaurant, even $ $106,000 is not bad for starting a business. The point is, it varies greatly. You need to do the math before spending any money so that you do not run out before you get started.

The numbers will also vary depending on your needs. Do you need an oven? A rotisserie? Coffee pots? A grill? Hot dog roller? The costs can range dramatically. Then, of course, you need to get and pay for all of the permits for the city/town you operate in, and board of health approval. There simply is no exact number, but you can be pretty sure the vehicle is your most expensive investment.

"For a beginner chef who wants to be an entrepreneur, or a chef who wants to downsize and make his life simple but still do what he loves to do, [a food truck] is a dream come true! This concept is simple and it's all about the net profit, not the gross!

save

Because a home office is not essential for this business, simply find a place in your home to quietly do the books and handle the payroll. And if you need some office equipment or furniture, look for used items or convert other furnishings into what you need.

Insurance Needs

Among the most important costs you will have is insurance. You need to cover both a business and a vehicle against as many potential risks as possible, especially if you are driving around with a few propane tanks strapped to your cart or truck. You need both liability and theft insurance. Review all other possibilities carefully, including those required by your state. You might even consider employment interruption insurance in case a natural disaster makes it impossible to do business.

Legal and Financial

Don't forget to set aside fees for an attorney and an accountant or bookkeeper to help you get your books set up. In all businesses, legal assistance and proper bookkeeping are vital. A business attorney will help you with contracts, setting up a business structure (LLC, corporation, etc.), and making sure you have met your business licensing requirements. Your accountant will set you up to handle local, state, and federal taxes as well as let you know what do and do not count as business expenses. Hint: Save your receipts when you buy anything for the business.

Operating Costs

Your operating costs are the expenses you pay regularly to keep your business up and running. Consider these as the monthly payments, although some will be made weekly. Your operating costs will be both fixed and variable. Fixed expenses are those you will pay every month, such as:

- Vehicle payments (unless you've purchased your vehicle outright)
- Vehicle rental
- Commercial kitchen rental (This may vary depending on the deal you sign and the frequency of use; caterers often start with more open-ended deals.)
- Vehicle parking expenses (or space rental expenses for a kiosk)
- Insurance

Variable expenses are those that will change with the flow and/or growth of the business. Variable expenses include:

- Food and/or ingredients
- Parking permits (such as for special events or corporate parties)
- Delivery or shipping (this can change depending on volume)
- Gas and oil
- Vehicle repairs
- Packaging, labels, etc.
- Marketing and promotion
- Miscellaneous (including parking tickets, which you should try to minimize to keep the law on your side)

Numerous factors including the weather (which may preclude you from outdoor selling in places like New England or Minnesota in January or February) as well as peak tourist seasons and changes in parking rules and fees will factor into the variability of your costs.

You need to estimate how much you need per month, which means doing some math. Expenses such as food need to be watched the most carefully. Add up your weekly bills, and then calculate your monthly food costs (at 4.3 weeks per month). Do the same with paper goods or anything you are buying on a weekly or frequent basis. Monthly bills are easy. However, variables such as marketing and promotion are tricky.

If, for example, you need $1,200 to promote yourself at two fairs and you need to pay the bills in March and September (at $600 each), those are spikes for those months that do not fall into your usual pattern. You'll want to know which months are more likely to have higher totals than others. This can help you plan in advance. If, however, you buy a piece of new equipment in June for $1,200, for tax purposes you may wish to amortize the expense of the equipment over the year, which would be $100 per month for 12 months. Discuss the advantages of this with your accountant.

Growing Pains

Rome wasn't built in a day, nor was the success of the Kogi BBQ Truck in Los Angeles. Businesses endure growing pains. Zack Brooks notes that it takes time to make a go of it in the industry, whether you are running a cart or a restaurant. "You need to have enough capital on hand to last at least six months to a year because it takes time to become profitable. The most successful trucks are the ones that have been doing it the longest."

The rule of thumb, in business, says that it takes most new businesses at least a couple of years to show a profit. The larger the investment in the business, the longer it may take. Having a lower overhead, you can cut this number down by developing a good working business model. This means a business model whereby you have carefully thought about every step of the business process so that you can streamline it to be cost effective and time efficient.

Volume

One of the key factors in the food industry is volume. First, this refers to how much you buy, and then how much you prepare and/or cook during your time in the kitchen. It also refers to how much you can sell during your sales hours. Unless you are a caterer being paid in advance for X number of ice cream cones, chicken enchiladas, or steaks, you have a limited amount of time during your business day to sell your inventory.

Natasha Usher, who ran the Lucinda Creperie truck in Jersey City, New Jersey, noted the importance of being prepared because your sales window of opportunity is limited. "We have lunch and dinner times, which gives us only about five or six hours in which to sell, unlike a restaurant where people can wander in at any time, so you have to be all prepared for those times of day," she explained. But she puts in ten hours a day of work when considering the preparation, travel time, and cleanup.

Because many foods do not keep well overnight, you typically need to sell what you bring—and bring as much as you can sell. The Catch 22 is that knowing how much to bring is dependant on how much you can sell, and you don't know that until you sell out. Even then, you don't know how much more you could have sold. "In the beginning a lot of this is trial and error," says Marcus Gotay of WHEDco, adding that after a while you get a feel for it and it becomes easier to judge.

Volume also depends on the foods that you sell. That's why hot dogs, kebobs, ice cream, tacos, enchiladas, pretzels, cookies, cupcakes, and similar foods have been favorites of food vendors for years. They are easy to carry in volume, keep warm or cool, and sell quickly. They are also tangible. It's easier to say "I sold 62 donuts today" than to figure out portion size. It is, for example, harder to calculate how much pasta you can and will serve in a day (and less easy to manage), which probably explains why you see very few spaghetti trucks.

You need to serve quickly in order to make your money because unlike a restaurant, your time frame is limited, so you need to make the most out of key times, such as 11:30 A.M. to 1:30 P.M., the lunch hours.

While caterers typically accept credit and debit cards as well as personal checks, the mobile food industry operates primarily in cash. On the positive side, this speeds up the process. On the negative side, you do not want to be carrying around a lot of cash, especially at night. Cart and truck owners have reported robberies. It is, therefore, important to have someone working with you, or whom you know and trust, do a bank run during the day to get some of the cash out of the vehicle.

> **tip**
>
> Some cart owners have a second licensed cart ready to take over for the first one should they run out of food. This can continue the flow of service, but you'll need to pay someone to get that second cart to your location. Make sure the profits outweigh the salary of your assistant.

Pricing

It all comes down to pricing! If your prices are too high, people will not buy your foods. If your prices are too low, you won't make any money. So establishing your price is extremely important. Many people in business learn the hard way, by losing money for a while before adjusting their prices.

With the exception of some of the gourmet food trucks crossing the price line and going up to $12 or $14 with specialty dishes, most mobile foods are priced at $10 or under. For catering, pricing is a different animal.

Pricing Principals

There are several factors to consider when determining your prices. For most familiar items, there are certain price points that customers will pay. You can typically get an idea of what they are by looking at various menus and doing some research. For example, a food cart or truck taco usually sells between $3 and $6, so you'll want to be within that range. Likewise, nobody is going to pay $6 for a water bottle (unless they are at a sports arena). The difference between charging $3 and $6 depends on a variety of factors, starting with whether or not you will see a profit when you factor in all of your costs. Below are some of the other determining factors, when it comes to pricing.

What a Customer Will Pay

What customers will pay is largely based on location and product demand. Someone in New York City will be accustomed to paying more for lunch than a person in Milwaukee. The affluence of a community and the lifestyle of the area(s) in which you serve both influence how much someone will pay for food. Some customers simply have more expensive tastes (literally), while others are on a tight budget and are more price conscious. The majority are willing to pay somewhere in between the common price points. Get to know which customers you will be serving.

Competitive Pricing

Take a look at what your competitors, or future competitors, are charging. Read various menus, particularly those posting foods you plan to serve. Make comparisons among like products. For example, compare chocolate chip cookies to chocolate chip cookies and not to oatmeal raisin cookies. Also look at portion sizes. If you've got the longer hot dog, you can charge more—yes, size matters.

You want to be competitively priced, which brings us back to those earlier price points. Of course, if you can price yourself below your competitors and still make a profit, that's great. If you are priced the same, then you need to wow customers with your food, your customer service, sense of community, or whatever else you've got above and beyond your competitors. Your advantage may simply be some good write-ups in the media or some great responses to your food on Twitter or Facebook.

Higher or Prestige Pricing

If you are charging more than what is in the common price range, you need to have a reason why. It might be that you are selling homemade, organic products while your competitor is selling a commercial brand. You can then promote your competitive edge and justify your prices based on having the organic, healthier product. Reasons for charging a little more also include:

- Special ingredients or unique combinations
- Fresh organic or farm-to-table ingredients
- Sides, such as chips with a sandwich
- Portion size, more for your money
- Convenience (If the next closest sushi cart or restaurant is a mile away, customers might not mind paying a little more.)

Your Profit Margin

It doesn't matter what kind of pricing system you use, if you are not making more money than you are spending, you will have to make adjustments. You may need to find suppliers with lower prices. You may need to buy in greater volume. This might mean starting a food co-op to bring the volume of food up and the prices down.

Buying is a major factor in pricing in the food industry. That is why restaurant owners, and mobile food vendors, like you, shop at places like Restaurant Depot (restaurantdepot.com), Jetro (jetro.com), or popular price clubs such as Costco (costco.com) or Sam's Club (samsclub.com).

Many people in the food business also find certain items that they buy from unique suppliers that add something special to a key menu item. For example, pastry caterer Celine, who started and owns Les Canelés de Céline, does most of her shopping at Costco. However, she buys specially made imported butter from France, and that is what distinguishes her pastries from those of her competition.

Caterers also need to determine the markup on their menu items largely based on their food costs as well as the cost of labor. In addition, they need to determine their costs for different-sized parties because prices when ordering vary based on volume and the number of employees will also vary. Using a tiered pricing structure, you can calculate the cost for different sized events. For example, the same party for 30 people might cost less per person for 60 people because you will not be paying twice as much for the food. However, you may then need to factor in the cost of a second server because typically you look for one server per 30 or 40 people. If, however, you are delivering but not serving the food, the cost should be less then having a server included. Unlike a food truck, where a taco is on the menu for $5, your costs can vary depending on additional factors. For example, with a server a dozen tacos may come to $5 each. Three dozen may bring your cost down to $4 each. Without factoring in a server, three dozen may be $3 each. Shrimp filling might bring the cost up to $6.50 each. While these are random numbers, they illustrate how a caterer has to price the same item based on quantity, having a server, and other factors.

Making Money

In the end, once you have determined your costs, you need to consider how many cookies, crepes, tacos, or portions you need to sell to overcome your list of expenses. Therefore, if your total monthly expenses average $3,000, you need to sell more than 600 tacos priced at $5 each per month to break even, or roughly 140 per week or 23 per day if you work six days a week. If you average selling 100 tacos a day, or bring in $500 a day, you will make $2,500 a week or roughly $10,000, 450 per month for a profit of $7,000 after expenses or over $84,000 per year. Of course, this doesn't factor in the $10,000 you spent the first year on your truck or the $10,000 in additional startup costs. It also doesn't factor in other items you may sell such as water bottles or other beverages. Remember, that first year is the toughest in which to turn a profit. Some vehicle owners report $400 a day in sales and others

The night crowd gathers at the Streetza Pizza truck in Milwaukee, Wisconsin.

claim $2,000 per day. It depends on factors such as your location, your food, your marketing, your pricing, and your reputation.

Of course, you may lose days, weeks, or even months in bad weather areas. Conversely, you may make up for this by taking on some catering jobs or selling products wholesale. As with any business, there are many factors that determine your success or failure. Some will be out of your control, but a lot will depend on your decisions and in this business your flexibility. Be ready to change your prices if you are losing money. However, if you are breaking even or making some profits in the beginning, have patience. Businesses need time to grow.

CHAPTER 10

Finding Funding

For decades, many immigrants trying to make money in a new homeland poured their hearts, souls, and savings into their food carts. Whether it was on the Lower East Side of Manhattan or along Coney Island, where hot dog vendors dotted the boardwalk, it was a means to an end, a way of making a living. Today, entrepreneurs are thinking big and looking for financial backers to help them in reaching their dreams of success in the mobile food industry.

First Do the Math

Once you have reviewed your startup costs and ongoing costs, as discussed in the previous chapter, you can determine what size business to start and how much financing you will need. If, for example, you have determined that all of your startup costs come to $35,000 (including the first month's expenses) and that your ongoing monthly costs are $4,000, you'll want at least five more months (six months total) costs on hand to get started. Thus you would need $59,000 to keep you afloat for six months if sales are not good initially ($35,000 + [6 months x 4,000 = $24,000] = $59,000). You might decide to seek $65,000 in financing to have some cash on hand. Cash flow is vital to any business. Always making sure to have some accessible cash is important, especially in a largely cash business.

Your business plan will explain how you plan to sell enough enchiladas to cover your monthly expenditure. You can outline your costs and your potential profits on an Excel spreadsheet and work with the numbers until you figure out a price at which you can realistically come out ahead. Of course your startup costs will disappear after the first year (unless you are paying off a vehicle over time), but remember, a realistic forecast for making a profit may take at least one year.

The cost of living varies from city to city as will the cost of doing business and your potential income. Of course no business is a sure thing. Once you have punched the numbers, and assuming you can find decent if not spectacular locations, you can determine how much you may need in outside funding to get you started.

Funding

If you are looking for financing, even from friends and family, you should have a completed business plan with the financial pages included. A profit and loss statement projecting your profits over one, three, and five years (hopefully showing growth) can provide an idea of how you see the business becoming more profitable over time. Beyond the numbers, you need to explain how your system and your plans will build your revenue. What do you envision for the future? Be realistic, but have plans to expand your menu, increase your base of locations, do additional marketing, etc. Investors want to see the profit potential of a business and know that you have thought it through. That's why a business plan or at least a business summary is so important.

Investors are more inclined to invest or lend you money if they see the plan on paper showing they can make a profit from investing or at least make their money back. After all, the age-old question from an investor remains: What's in it for me?

Sources for business funding include:

- Your personal savings
- Friends, neighbors, and relatives
- Assets
- Bank or credit unions loans
- Outside investors (including angels and venture capitalists)

tip

Keep in mind that the modern day business plan need not be numerous pages, and may run 20 pages tops, or even be shown to potential investors in a well planned PowerPoint demonstration.

Personal Savings

If you have money saved and set it aside for opening a business, you can determine if it is enough to start the business on your own.

If you have not been saving up specifically to open a business, you will need to prioritize your upcoming personal and family needs and then determine how much savings are left over after paying for necessities. Paying off debts is especially important before going into business.

It is not recommended that you dip into retirement savings or borrow against your credit cards, especially in a shaky economy. Savings used to start a business should be earmarked as such or so should money you can afford beyond paying off your debts and taking care of the needs of your family.

Friends and Relatives

Partnering and borrowing money are quite different. Dining has long been associated with families and today many food businesses, from restaurants to mobile food vehicles, are owned and operated by husband and wife teams or families. For instance, Van Leeuwen Artisan Ice Cream is owned by two brothers and the wife of one of the brothers.

Any kind of partnership needs a breakdown of responsibilities. If one person enjoys cooking while the other enjoys handling the marketing and production aspects of the business, then you are all set. Such partnerships, in which each person meets a different need, are typically the most successful. In all instances business papers should be drawn up to indicate who gets what if the family members go separate ways. Of course this is not always the case, and friction or bad blood is the result. Make sure to spell everything out in advance so you don't end up playing the blame game.

Many non-spousal partners also team up to run food businesses. In all cases partnership agreements should be drawn up with an attorney and signed. You'll be grateful later. It's important to spell out the specifics of the agreement. For example, one partner may be providing money but not taking part in the day-to-day operations of the business. Does she have a say in key business decisions? Is she a silent partner?

warning

Don't slice up the pie too many ways. Too many lenders can become confusing (as well as meddlesome). Try to borrow from as few people as possible.

Once you decide, put it into the agreement. Think of all the issue that may emerge and cover them in advance. If either partner feels that he will be resentful later on, speak up in advance and talk through the potential problems. The need for business partnership agreements cannot be overemphasized.

Borrowing funding from a friend or relative is a different ballgame. Again, you need to draw up an agreement, but this should be a monetary agreement, meaning money is lent to be repaid on a certain schedule or by a certain date, perhaps with interest. The biggest concern when borrowing money from friends or family is straining the relationship. Therefore, you need to treat such a loan as you would treat a bank loan and write out some terms about paying back the loan.

Seek people who believe in your business goals and will be supportive. Also seek people who will not expect that they have a controlling interest in how you run your business for their investment dollars.

Assets

If you already own a business, selling it or selling part of it can bring you some capital. If you do not need the money for bailing yourself out of debt or for other immediate needs, this is a great way to finance your new venture. Many new mobile food entrepreneurs sell off part of another business venture to buy their first cart or truck.

You may also have personal assets that you can part with to start up a new business, such as the antique car in your driveway or some old baseball cards worth $5,000.

Recently married couples have sold off one of their two homes once they began cohabitating, while others have rented out their old singles pad to bring in money.

Banks or Credit Unions

Banks, credit unions, and other lending institutions have long been the primary source for money for small businesses. If you are looking for business loans from commercial

tip

Contact at least one of the big three credit bureaus for your credit scores:

1. Equifax: 1-800-685-1111, PO Box 740241, Atlanta, GA 30374 (equifax.com)

2. Experian: 1-888-397-3742, PO Box 2002, Allen, TX 75013 (experian.com)

3. TransUnion: 1-800-888-4213, PO Box 2000, Chester, PA 19022 (transunion.com)

lenders, you need to have your financial matters in order. Commercial lenders want to know that you are a good risk.

A good credit rating is essential in order to demonstrate that you will be able to pay the loan back promptly. Before you start on your quest for money, it's a good idea to check on your credit score at the three major credit bureaus. Then you will know where you stand.

Read your credit reports over very carefully, especially if your rating is not as good as you expected it to be. Credit bureaus make more mistakes than you would ever imagine. Make sure there are no errors on your credit reports. If there are errors, have them corrected.

It's important to get your credit scores in order before seeking a loan. You'll need to start paying off any and all outstanding debts and get to a point where you can open a new credit card or take out a small loan and pay it back promptly, showing you are on solid financial ground. Never go to places that can "magically repair bad credit." Remember, anything that seems too good to be true is usually a major risk. You are very likely to find yourself in a worse situation than you were in before.

Several factors come into play when obtaining a loan from a bank or a credit union. The economic climate, your track record in business, and your credit rating are most significant.

Lending institutions want to know that you are a sound credit risk. They will also want to know exactly what your future plans are beyond simply "opening a food business." This is where your detailed business plan comes in handy. Have people you know and trust look at your business plan to see that it makes sense. Your business experience should be included in your business plan. If it is not, make sure you highlight exactly what you have done before that makes you the ideal person to open such a business and run it successfully.

tip

Always invest some of your own money into your business, even if you have to secretly borrow it from mom and pop. Lenders and outside investors look much more favorably on a business owner if he is "standing" there with them, taking the same risk. They figure that if you are willing to put your own money into this venture then you will stand behind it and take it much more seriously.

You need to put up collateral for the loan. Carefully consider assets that you can use for collateral. Avoid putting your home on the line. If you haven't run a business before, keep in mind that you can always start small on a shoestring budget from savings or loans from friends and/or family, then run the business for a short time before approaching a bank or credit union. This will show that you are seriously trying to make a go of the business. People have started food carts for under $5,000 and run them successfully, showing profits. They have then asked for and received small loans to upgrade to a small truck or simply make improvements to the cart. Loans or getting a commercial line of credit can be used for business improvements. Spell out the need for and cost of the improvements you have in mind.

Outside Investors: Angels and Venture Capitalists

You may also look for outside investors to help you launch and even maintain your new business. Venture capital is the term for the money you are seeking. A well-constructed business plan and a good presentation are necessary to interest such investors. Because you, or you and your partner, are at the core of this business, the emphasis will be on what you have to offer in terms of experience, know-how, dedication, feel for business, marketing skills, passion, and of course good food. It's not only what is on paper but also your presentation that needs to be polished. You want to be able to convey your passion for this endeavor and your commitment (remember, investing your own money is important) if you want to be taken seriously. You also need to be ready to answer all possible questions, politely and without hesitation.

How long do you think it will be before you see a profit? Answer the question and have the paperwork ready, as discussed earlier, with your one-, three-, and five-year projections.

Consider questions such as:

- If you are sick, who runs the cart?
- What locations have you determined are best for your truck?
- How much markup can you make per sale?

- (For a mobile caterer) Do you have a maximum order you can handle and what is that maximum?

The point is that for financial backing in any business you need to figure out all of the particulars in advance and be ready to answer whatever questions are asked with confidence. Hint: Don't ramble. Short answers with good explanations or specific examples will suffice.

The most significant concerns for investors are whether YOU can make this business happen and whether YOU are responsible, trustworthy, and able to run a team and sell a product. The more domain expertise you can show the better: Have you run a restaurant before? Have you sold anything to consumers as a vendor? Run a store? Run a food truck? You need to stand out because the business revolves around your vision.

Also, consider what you are giving this investor in exchange for his capital. Remember, it's not a donation, it's an investment, a risky investment, and investors want to know what their upside is. How are they going to get their money back and then some! You need to know how you are set up to do this. Is it a profit share? Stock? Both? Work with your accountant and/or a business advisor in advance to determine the best way to repay investors.

Anyone could be a potential outside investor. However, if you are seeking more significant funding, such as $50,000 or $100,000, you may be looking for a venture capitalist or an angel investor. A venture capitalist is someone in the business of seeking investment opportunities, who provides capital for either a business startup or expansion. Typically, venture capitalists seek a higher rate of return than they would receive in other, more traditional, investments. They may be looking for upwards of 25 percent, which means that most small businesses do not go this route.

Angel investors, however, are people looking to back business ventures in hopes of making a profit down the road. Typically their expectations are not as high as venture capitalists. Many angel investors are busy working in their own fields or retired and seeking outside investments. In some cases an angel investor will provide expert advice, while in other cases she will serve as a silent backer.

tip

Develop your elevator pitch, a very concise pitch that defines your business idea briefly, explaining the business, the costs, your background, and why this business can work. An elevator pitch, typically 30 seconds, is designed to be told to a captive investor in the time it takes to ride up in an elevator. Near the end of the 1988 movie *Working Girl*, Melanie Griffith gives her pitch to the major investors in an elevator and wins them over by presenting a very sound and logical business proposal in roughly 30 seconds. That's how it's done.

Your Presentation: Make It Mouthwatering

The keys to your presentation to investors lie in the following questions:

- *Why is this a good idea?*

  Are you the first falafel truck in Portsmouth, New Hampshire? The only truck to sell homemade fresh ice cream in Seattle? The first truck to make Mexican food with a Korean twist and market it in a largely Korean neighborhood? Are you the first mobile caterer to provide Hawaiian Luaus in office parks?

  The point is to illustrate what sets you apart from being just another business. Is it a great location, a unique menu, or perhaps the timing is right for your food to reach a certain demographic region. Do plenty of market research.

- *Who are you?*

  Just another person who wants to get into a hot business is not a good answer. Are you a great cook? (Bring food along.) Are you a great marketer? Do you cook and market? Do you have a head for business? Are you great at managing the many details that go into such an endeavor? Are you a people person?

  Let investors learn to love you, but don't overdo it. Be yourself, not a character.

- *What makes your food so good?*

  Is it fresh from the farm? Homemade? Have a special "secret" ingredient? Food combinations never tasted before? Be honest and passionate about your food, but don't overdo it.

- *What is your marketing plan?*

  A few great locations? Promoting your catering company to party planners all over the city? Using Twitter and social media? Will you provide entertainment? The point is, let them know your plan for getting customers or clients.

- *What's in it for Me?*

  And remember, show them the money—or where it will come from in the end. Be realistic.

  And don't provide pie in the sky answers, even if you plan to open a Pie in the Sky food truck.

> **tip**
>
> It's hard to find angel investors and/or venture capitalists. You might visit funding post.com, a business that arranges for special VC and Angel showcases in various parts of the country. You sign up and pay to attend such an event at which up-and-coming entrepreneurs, like you, get to meet with many angel investors and VCs in one place. Have your short elevator pitch ready and demonstrate the enthusiasm you have for your business venture.

In the end, make sure you let backers or investors know where you plan to spend their money and be as transparent in business as possible. Transparency is a very popular term in business circles today. Basically, it means letting people know what you are up to and if something goes awry, acknowledging it and letting them know how you plan to fix any such problems before they become points of contention. Transparency builds trust, and trust builds a strong reputation in the business community.

Franchising

There are literally thousands of franchises in the United States, including many in the food industry. As the mobile food industry continues to thrive, more food franchises will provide entrepreneurs with additional business opportunities. The concept of franchising is based on a parent company, such as McDonald's or Subway, offering ownership of their business model to entrepreneurs in other parts of the country. The result is that entrepreneurs get to own and run a local business that is part of a large, typically successful, proven entity.

Perhaps the best-known franchised food trucks come from Mister Softee, which first showed up in 1956 with soft ice cream and frozen treats. Initially sold from ice cream stands, the company decided it could best reach more customers by taking its ice cream to the streets. So, with a catchy jingle to attract attention, off they went. Today, with more than 600 trucks and 350 franchise dealers, Mister Softee is the largest franchiser of soft ice cream trucks in the United States.

The Pros and Cons of Franchising

Some entrepreneurs start looking for a franchise that sells a food or beverage of interest to them. Others seek opportunities based on the initial cost and requirements. Franchises, especially the most successful ones, usually make all of their requirements for becoming an owner (aka a franchisee) available.

The big plus of franchising is that you get name recognition. Starting a new business means having to establish yourself and build a brand from scratch. Having a well-known name can immediately draw customers. You also have a tried-and-true product, which means you can open more quickly, without having to go through the long process of creating and developing your food items. Buying a cart or kiosk of a well-known coffee company, for example, means you are selling a proven product from a company familiar to your target audience. Of course location will still be a factor in your success, but in many cases, such as with express food kiosks, the franchising company will have already done the research and scouted locations. In short, owning a franchise jumps you ahead in the process of opening a new business, letting you bypass much of the trial-and-error stage.

In addition, with sufficient support and guidance, as a franchisee you should not have to re-invent the wheel, so to speak, by doing everything yourself. Most franchises have working systems in place for running the business. As a result, franchise owners do not have to wait nearly as long to see a steady stream of income.

The biggest drawback to starting a franchise is the price. Franchise fees and overall investments can run to $100,000 and up, although some food carts can be much less. While you will see income more quickly, you may still be waiting for a profit because your initial startup cost is higher than starting up your own food cart or truck business. Also, before you start, there are financial requirements, such as total net worth and liquidity that you must meet. Then after you have started, franchises typically require you to pay royalties, perhaps 5 to 10 percent, of gross sales.

Another serious concern in buying a franchise is the franchise license agreement. It is imperative that you read and understand the entire contract. Having an attorney review it is strongly advised because there is usually a lot of fine print to decipher.

One major negative for many new business owners, especially food truckers is the lack of freedom. You are essentially playing by someone else's rules. While you own the cart, kiosk, or truck, the franchise company has a say in how things are done. Therefore, if you want to be creative and march to your own drummer, franchising is not for you. As it turns out, one of the reasons why there are not a lot of franchised food trucks is because many truck owners are foodies with a passion for creativity. Ironically, it is also a business in which many customers like the novelty and creativity of their favorite trucks. Scott Basinger of Milwaukee's Streetza Pizza truck recalls a truck from Toppers Pizza, a Midwestern food chain, pulling up right near their truck. "At first I was worried that they would take all of our business, but as it turned out, people were more interested in what we had to offer since we were new and original and Toppers was something they could get at many locations in Milwaukee."

The upside of a franchise is that it lets you start a business more quickly and jump in with much of the preliminary work already done. It eliminates much of the risk of a brand new business and gives you name recognition and a tried-and-true product. Most franchises provide training and support, while many also offer financial assistance and payment plans. It is also easier to get funding for a franchise because of the proven business (of course you need to prove that you can run it).

Just remember that all of this comes at a higher price and will limit your creativity as you are in the business world not merely as an owner but also as part of a bigger business universe. So you do need to weigh the pros and cons carefully.

The franchise possibilities when it comes to mobile food vendors has remained primarily with some of the larger players and those, like Mister Softee, that have been established. Individual truck owners have tried to expand through franchising opportunities, but most have come up short.

Overall, thus far, franchising has been a hit or miss proposition with some trucks like The Sauca Truck in Washington, DC giving it a go and later closing down the operation while Cousins Maine Lobster Truck, which opened in Los Angeles in 2012, took off so quickly that within couple years franchising has led to a second truck in Phoenix and brand new trucks in Dallas, Houston, Las Vegas, Orlando, and other locations for an initial investment between $146,300 and $192,900.

A familiar food truck problem that comes into play when franchising is that the rules, regulations, and laws vary from city to city and region to region from food preparation to licenses to parking. Unlike brick-and-mortar franchises like Subway or Denny's, most food trucks are not very well known names, so it's important to tap into well established food truck markets.

Finding a Franchise

While there are not a significant number of franchised food trucks or even carts, do not despair, there are a lot of franchises when it comes to kiosks. There are a number of well-known food companies that are already franchising express kiosks. You may have seen mall-sized kiosk versions of Baskin-Robbins or Ben & Jerry's. These are franchised.

To find franchise opportunities, you can start on the internet. Entrepreneur has an annual listing of the top 500 U.S. franchises. Many of the food businesses listed include express kiosks (entrepreneur.com/franchise500/index.html). Franchise Gator (franchisegator.com) and Franchise Solutions (franchisesolutions.com) are other websites that can help you look by industry or by state for franchise opportunities. They include information such as the liquid capital necessary and the total capital investment required. Sites such as these provide a way to narrow down the vast number of possibilities to a few based on your own criteria. You can also select a company (such as Mister Softee at mistersoftee.com/franchise-opportunities) go directly to the website, to look at Franchise Opportunities.

Companies to consider for kiosks, express, or, in some cases, even trucks, include:

- Auntie Anne's Soft Pretzels
- Bahama Buck's Original Shaved Ice Cream
- Baskin-Robbins
- Ben & Jerry's
- Big Apple Bagels/My Favorite Muffin
- Blimpie Subs and Salads
- Famous Chicken 'n Biscuits
- Calexico Restaurants & Food Carts
- California Quivers (a fresh fruit ice company also franchising carts)
- Camille's Ice Cream

- Captain Tony's Pizza and Pasta Emporium
- Carvel
- Cheeseburger Cheeseburger
- Chester's Chicken
- Cinnabon
- Coffee Beanery
- Cousins Maine Lobster
- Cousins Subs
- Deli Delicious Premium Deli Sandwiches
- Denny's
- Dippin' Dots
- Dunn Bros Coffee
- East Coast Wings
- Fatburger North America
- Figaro's Pizza
- French Fry Heaven
- Fresh Healthy Café
- Golden Krust Caribbean Bakery & Grill

Ten Things to Look for in a Franchise

1. A familiar franchise name and brand
2. Popular consumer products
3. A high-traffic location
4. Minimal labor requirements
5. Year-round sales continuity
6. Reasonable fees and commissions
7. Training
8. Ongoing support
9. A positive working relationship with the franchising company
10. A fair franchise agreement

- Great American Cookies
- Great Steak & Potato
- The Greene Turtle Sports Bar and Grille
- Groucho's Deli
- Haagen-Daz
- Juice It Up!
- Kolache Factory
- Kona Ice
- Lee's Hoagie House
- Logic In A Cup Espresso
- Maui Wowi Hawaiian Coffees and Smoothies
- Menchie's (self serve frozen yogurt)
- Nathan's Famous Inc. (Hot dogs, hamburgers, etc.)
- Nestle Toll House Cafe by Chip
- Orange Leaf Frozen Yogurt
- The Original SoupMan
- Orion Food Systems (fast food systems for nontraditional markets)
- Paciugo Gelato Caffe
- Philly Pretzel Factory
- Pinkberry Ventures (frozen yogurt and yogurt shakes)
- Pizza Factory
- Potatopia Franchise
- Pretzelmaker
- Quesada Burritos—Tacos
- Red Mango—Frozen Yogurt and Juice Bar
- Repicci's Italian Ices
- Rita's Italian Ice
- Robeks Fresh Juices and Smooties
- Russo's (pizza, pasta, salads, sandwiches)
- Scooper's Ice Cream
- Smoothie King
- Sub Zero Ice Cream
- Subway
- Surf City Squeeze
- Taco Bell
- Taste of Mediterranean

- TCBY and Mrs. Fields
- Tropical Smoothie Café
- Waffle Brothers
- Wetzel's Pretzels
- Which Wich Superior Sandwiches
- Yogurt Fruz
- Yummie Cupcakes

(Listings Courtesy of Entrepreneur's 2015 Top 500 Franchises)

These are just some companies that list the express/kiosk as a franchise possibility. Each one will have its own system in place and a franchise agreement spelling out the details, including the franchise fee, overall investment cost, etc.

Franchise Brokers

When looking for a franchise, another option is to contact a franchise broker. As is the case with most industries, someone has come along to serve as the middle person to help you find a franchise opportunity. Such a broker can help you narrow down the possibilities and make a wise choice. The sheer volume of potential franchises is mind numbing. You've already narrowed down the field to the food industry and narrowed it down again to a kiosk or mobile business. Nonetheless, some individuals, as well as some parent companies, are more comfortable working through a franchise broker.

Do Your Homework

You want to see which franchisers offer franchisees, like yourself, the best opportunity to own a successful business. Franchise owners have worked long and hard to build their name, recognition, and brand, so they are very protective and will restrict and control areas such as advertising and marketing, training, insurance, cleanliness, corporate image, the suppliers you may use, etc. This is their way of protecting themselves. Conversely, you need to protect yourself as some franchises can make life difficult for their own franchisees. For this reason, you want to check out a franchise thoroughly and talk to other franchisees.

You want to look for franchises that:

- Provide training and marketing
- Describe in detail what will and will not be provided by the franchise company
- Offer good financing terms
- Provide a detailed list of all fees that you will be charged

Licensing: Here's How It's Done

If you do something well, why not share It with others … while making money off of it as well. Licensing can let you do that with far less paperwork than franchising.

If you want to license your brand, the first step—and it may take some time and a little more hard work—is to build your brand. You want other people to be attracted to your truck because the brand is familiar and attractive. Many trucks have created a local brand and built a following. They have a distinct personality and therefore, when the truck shows up, people are drawn to it because of the sense of familiarity. For example, if you see a Mister Softee or a Starbucks truck, you immediately know what you are getting. It's all about selling the brand.

To license your brand, you first need to:

○ Establish a reputation for consistent, quality food, service, and personality.

○ Have a limited menu—don't try to be a little bit of everything.

○ Provide something that gives you a competitive edge—what makes your truck different than everyone else's?

○ Maintain a low overhead, so licensees won't be intimidated.

○ Market yourself everyplace! From Facebook, to local newspapers, get your name out there. Remember, licensing is largely about familiarity.

In the end, you are not franchising a full operating system but licensing a brand. Licensees should have more creativity and flexibility, but you want them to uphold your good name. A brand is about reliability, trust, quality, and consistency. Sure, a licensee can add menu items and work on a different schedule depending on the most profitable possibilities in their town or city, but you want licensees to follow your lead. With that in mind, it's advisable to start by licensing in a nearby city or town (obviously not in your usual territory) so that word of your success can help them get their marketing strategy off the ground.

You should also offer licensees access to the vault, so to speak, with a wealth of knowledge on areas including: marketing strategy, social media strategy, sales strategy, sales forecasts, projected cash flow (6 months), and so on. You want them to succeed. They help you build your brand on a regional, perhaps national, level while you help them get their business started—it's a win win.

- Are transparent and provide sufficient company information
- Allow you to talk to other franchisees (this should be part of transparency)
- Offer clear dispute resolution procedures that are not markedly in favor of the franchiser (such as requiring you to attend arbitration hearings only in the state of the franchise company's headquarters)
- Offer you the same or a similar renewal contract (if they offer them at all)
- Provide an early-out provision in the contract if the franchiser/franchisee do not have a good working relationship
- Provide a clear and detailed procedure for you to sell or transfer ownership without having to waive your ownership rights to the franchiser
- Protect your territorial exclusivity

Eric Stites, founder and CEO of Franchise Business Review (franchisebusiness review.com), another good source for anyone interested in learning more about franchises, stresses the importance of talking to some franchisees before signing a franchise agreement. This can provide you with the inside track, letting you know how these business owners feel they have been treated.

Licensing: Adding Your Own Personal Touches

It's all up to the company, but some franchisers will let you add your own flavor to the décor, while others will be more strict. In some cases, licensing a name and brand from another company may be a better option. Licensing provides you with greater flexibility to run the business as you choose, within the general provisions of the license. Companies monitor the use of their name and brand, but are not involved in the actual day-to-day operations of the business. Typically their concern is centered on maintaining the value of the licensed brand, product, or service. The cost of licensing is significantly less than franchising. Unfortunately there are fewer licensing options available.

Naturally, there will be licensing agreements that are very transparent and appealing and others that do not provide the whole picture or all of the necessary help and guidance that you require. As is the case with a franchise agreement, you'll need to read over a licensing agreement very closely with an attorney familiar with such business documents.

▲

Franchising Your Business

You may consider launching your own mobile food or catering business with hope of franchising in the future. To do so, you will need to establish a recognizable brand and make sure to trademark everything you create in the process of building your business. A smooth running, easy-to-duplicate operating process that you have created and own is the key to your success, along with quality food, a catchy name, a logo, and a proven marketing plan. In other words, you need a business model that will entice new entrepreneurs to pay to replicate what you are doing. This takes time to establish and a lawyer who is familiar with franchising contracts to draw up the papers. Franchising a business is a time-consuming process and your legal fees can be high.

The idea of franchising or licensing your business is a marvelous long-range plan. It is something to strive for and requires you pay close attention to each step as you build your business. Write down exactly what you have done and how you have done it. Learn from mistakes you have made, and update your own business plan as you go. This way, once you have reached a point where your business is thriving, you can look back at how you reached your goal and market your knowledge, experience—and your brand—to others.

The Savvy Entrepreneur

One approach to building a business in conjunction with an established business is to take another brick-and-mortar business to the street. For this to work, you should have your business plan ready with one element to fill in, your menu items. This is where you approach successful brick-and-mortar businesses in your area with the idea of taking their food to the streets and promoting their business(es). Because food carts and trucks are still a popular trend, you'll want to arm yourself with a slew of articles about the industry, especially how popular it is in your area.

Such an arrangement could be beneficial for both parties. It supplies the foods and the popular name locally and eats some of your costs, while you find good locations where customers will eat their foods. Of course you have to work out a deal whereby you both make money. It can benefit the restaurant because your cart or truck serves as a billboard for the business.

Having a cart at the ready may be the more cost-effective way to make this work, depending on the food in question. Your goal, however, is to introduce the idea, explain how you will be marketing a company's yogurt or ice cream, baked goods, or smoothies, and have its logo and signage. In essence, you become the mobile arm of the business for a fee and/or cut of what you sell. Having great locations in mind can make this work very well. Also, make sure you draft a contract that benefits both sides with a win-win agreement.

Such a plan to bring a business to the streets takes time to put together. You will need to show why you are the person for the job. However, with a bit of salesmanship, you can team with a business to launch its products and share in the costs of the operation.

tip

If you take a mobile cart out for an up-and-coming company, find locations where its product is not yet on the shelves of local stores. This way you will not be competing with the local merchants. Have it in the contract that if the local merchant then sees your success and orders two-dozen boxes, essentially taking away your location, you get a cut because you helped make the deal happen.

CHAPTER 12

Moving On

Michelle Lozuaway who, along with her husband, Josh Lanahan, ran the very successful Fresh Local food truck in Portsmouth, New Hampshire, decided to sell the and move on to their own restaurant to serve the same "healthy street food". Having one of the top ten food trucks in the country. According to an article in *GQ* magazine, they were proud of their accomplishments as they brought street food to an area unfamiliar with the mostly urban phenomenon. The couple had already run a restaurant in Portsmouth and knew the lay of the land. So they bought a used 1986 truck, retrofitted it, and were off and running. "The truck paid for itself in one year, so it didn't cost us anything more," says Michelle, who enjoyed the food truck experience very much. Of course the fact that Josh was, and still is, a professional chef and Michelle took a cooking vacation in France, helped the business succeed and also helped them when it came time to transition to a restaurant setting.

The couple loved their seacoast New England community and enjoyed bringing street food to tourists and natives alike, but after losing battles to harsh winter weather, which makes life very difficult for street food vendors in the northern states, they decided to pursue their dream and opened STREET—Eat 360°, which serves a host of interesting options such as Korean Fried Chicken or the "Seamita," a combination of scallop, shrimp, and white fish cake with all the cemita fixin's, avocado, mexican fried cheese, onion, cilantro, and chipotle mayonnaise on a sesame bun or a Porchetta, a juicy Italian–style slow roasted herb garlic pulled pork sandwich with arugula and sharp provolone.

Selling a food truck, trailer, or cart is not uncommon, as evidenced by the many used models on the road today. There is a lot of work in running a mobile food operation, and people burn out. At that point they are either making enough money to hire others to run the show or they decide to sell the truck and move on. Those who have been successful often move into restaurants in some capacity, either as a chef, a partner in an existing venture, or like Michelle and Josh, as owners of a new eatery. Others sell the truck, buy a smaller van, and move to catering exclusively or to the food manufacturing business. Cody and Kristen Fields from Austin's Mmmpanadas truck are not yet selling their truck, but they have found a steady location where it stays on a full-time basis. They are now working to expand their growing wholesale empanadas business.

Selling Your Business

Selling a food cart, kiosk, truck, trailer, or even a bus is one possibility. The other option, if your business has built a following and/or established a brand, is selling the business. There is a difference, one is a vehicle (or kiosk) and the other is all that goes into the business. If, for example, the Kogi BBQ were to go up for sale as businesses, the buyers would be buying the entire culture, mystique, and business associated with the trucks.

If you have built a brand, you have to decide whether you want to sell the vehicle and maintain your business name, intellectual properties, brand, and so on or sell all of the above. This depends on your future plans. Certainly if you are taking your popular cupcake business to a larger truck or your famous fried chicken from a cart to a small storefront, you will want to keep your name, logo, and everything else and sell only the vehicle. If you choose to sell a vehicle, you can browse some among the many classified ads and compare your vehicle to other similar ones in your region. For example, you may see an ad such as:

4/27/2014 (Ann Arbor, Michigan) Homemade Ice Cream Trailer with 1997 GMC stock truck. Includes 20-gallon ice cream maker with 2001 JD 5hp hit and miss engine on a wagon, sliding glass door freezer, 2 door cooler, 21 cubic ft. Frigidaire chest freezer, folding canopy, 30" x 48" commercial grade wagon, two hole sinks, outside sink, water heater, backflow valve, electrical plugs, anything you might need to get started. Call Marvin at xxx-xxx-xxxx for more information.

If you were selling a similar vehicle, you could call Marvin to get an idea of the price to see if your selling price was in the same general area.

Among the many sites to visit, you can check out the ads on eBay under food trucks, or go to festivals-and-shows.com to find both used trucks and trailers. By searching the internet you will find other sites that post similar ads.

Getting a Proper Valuation

If you are selling your entire mobile food business, name, brand, logo, and customer base, you want to get a fair valuation. So you need to start planning well in advance. Selling a mobile food business is much like selling a restaurant, except location can vary depending on the new owner's preference.

You need to start by documenting how your business is run, from your ongoing cost of supplies and your other expenses through your weekly sales. You also have overnight parking, an off site kitchen lease (if you need an off-site facility in your jurisdiction), and other things in place. These can be part of the deal, or not. The key is to prove the value of the business and have records for at least six months to show consistency. Nobody is going to buy a business based on a few good weeks.

Save receipts from your suppliers or vendors and copies of other expenses. Show sales totals for each day. Have your recent tweets from regular customers, and show the pages of the website. Illustrating that you have a loyal following can play a factor in the value of the business.

The truck itself also needs to be clean, and everything needs to be in top working condition. If you need to replace some older items, do so. It just like fixing up any vehicle for sale—having working parts counts!

It also helps to show that the business has been paying taxes and has been maintaining accurate books. Of course you should do this regardless of whether you are selling the business. You also want to show that you are not in debt. If you are paying off any equipment, let it be known if the buyer is picking up any debts you own.

An easy transition is also a plus when selling a business. The more you can make it a turn-key operation so that the new owners can step right in and get started quickly, the more appealing it will be to buyers who want to purchase an existing food business. After all, if your truck disappears from sight for a while, it will be much harder to pick up the momentum when the business returns to the streets.

If you have recipes written down and basic instructions as to how you run the daily operation, it can bode well for a new owner. However, you can also remind the new owners that they can put in their own touches as they see fit because it will be their business to run. For example, when a Jersey City couple purchased a food truck serving Mexican favorites the owner even sold them the recipes and showed the couple how to cook them. But, after a while, the couple wanted to put their own stamp on the business and decided instead to sell crepes. While they acknowledged that they might have made more money selling the popular Mexican food, they wanted to bring their crepes to the public, which they did successfully for a while before selling the truck and moving on to other endeavors.

You need to determine how much you are selling, and if you get a fair price, it's time to let go, even if it means your marvelous meatballs will now be replaced by grilled cheese sandwiches. One good place to post is on http://us.businessesforsale. com. An ad for such a business, including truck and route, priced at $35,000 may look like this:

Popular 2008 lunch truck with all the shelving, two freezers, storage and signage. Route included—16 regular locations—truck runs from 6:00 A.M. to 2:00 P.M. Two construction site stops alone bring in $200 a day each. Call now at . . .

While the idea of a mobile food business as a brand and not just a cart or truck is a rather new concept, the sale of a restaurant has been either a building and/or a business for years. Popular restaurants change ownerships but maintain the name and style that has built a lasting following. Less successful restaurants may sell the property, and let the new owner do as he or she pleases.

To sell, you will need to network and spread the word that the business is being put up for sale. From your followers to mobile food magazines and websites, you'll want to talk to people who actually get it and are part of the new street food culture. This helps you look for buyers who can appreciate the business and helps you advertise accordingly. Not unlike a restaurant sale, you should hire an attorney to work on the sales agreement. You also need to be patient.

Setting a Sales Price

First look at comparable vehicles of the same year and make as your cart, truck, or trailer to check prices. Then consider the condition of the vehicle as it relates to comparable vehicles. Then set your price up or down as you think reasonable.

Because it is not mobile, location counts for a kiosk. If you have an agreement with a location and a relationship with the mall or airport that your buyer can step into, that counts for something as well. If you are selling a franchised express-kiosk, you have to abide by the franchise agreement regarding a sale and work in conjunction with the franchise company or sell it back to them.

When pricing a business, your vehicle, other tangible items, and any intangibles such as a loyal following and popular brand are all used to set the price. After determining what your truck and equipment sell for, say $25,000, you need to measure the daily sales of your product. You will want to get a good estimate of how much of your sales are coming from regular customers. For example, if you can show that 20 percent your overall income, or $15,000, comes from regular customers, you will then want to add that to the sales price of your tangible assets. Therefore, if the tangibles, such as the truck and equipment, would sell for $25,000, you will add on the $15,000 that your regular customers will now bring to the new owner and ask for a sales price of $40,000.

All of this is what you need to calculate to come up with a valuation of your business. If you've worked long and hard at your recipes and at building up your following, don't sell yourself short. Some of the more popular food truck businesses today could easily sell for well over $100,000 because their brands are popular and customers seek them out. If that is you, all you need to do is prove how much business your truck brings in and what percentage is attributable to your brand, reputation, reviews, and the quality of your food—so keep good records.

If you own a catering business, your client list is your top asset. A truck is a truck, but the value of the list and the number of regular clients need to be calculated and sold accordingly because it would take a buyer much more time to compile a list of regular customers and a plan for the business than it would to simply find a van or truck.

Your recipes and kitchen skills are also part of the deal and need to be factored in. What is your value to the business, and how much is your knowledge and experience worth? This needs to be part of the equation. You also need to know the going rate for a kitchen space (if you own it) and try to gauge a fair price.

In any sale, remember to see how many potential buyers you get before selling. As is always the case, supply and demand count. The more in demand a catering business is in your area, the more money you can get.

▲

Finding Buyers

Word of mouth and social media are two ways of spreading the word that you are selling your business. Because you are mobile, a sign on your vehicle can generate a buyer's attention. Classified ads and web advertising can also be effective.

Placing classified in newspapers or on websites is a very common means of making a sale. Because word count is typically limited, sum up the highlights of the business in a few key words. Provide phone and email means of reaching you. Return calls promptly. Have answers at the ready for common questions, such as miles on the truck, equipment included, or the size of the van, or trailer. If people want to see what you are selling, meet them in a public place where you have room to park and talk—never let them take your truck for a spin unless you are sitting there with them and make sure they have a valid driver's license.

> **warning** ⚠
>
> Because many buyers cannot pay the full amount in cash, business sales often include the owner (you) getting part of the money up front and a note saying the buyer will pay the rest in regular payments. Make sure your note is legally binding (have a lawyer involved), and make sure the buyer puts up collateral of value (beyond the business assets) in case the buyer defaults on the loan.

Staying Involved, or Not

If you are selling and moving on to other endeavors, you can make a smooth transition and be on your way once the business is sold. If, however, you want to remain involved you can include such a plan in the sales agreement that will have you remaining as the cook or in some other role. This may not suit some buyers, but others may see the benefit of having you around to teach them the ropes. You have to work this out so you do not overstay your welcome. You also have to accept that you are no longer the boss but simply providing ideas or food. Another option is to stick around to simply help the new owner(s) through the transition period and then move on. Many former business owners see such a transition period as a means of closure.

And Finally

No matter whether you venture into the mobile food business with a part-time cart or a full-time bustaurant, there are a lot of factors that go into starting, running, and making a profit in this business. The most important things to remember are:

- Don't do this if you expect to get rich. Some mobile food entrepreneurs have made a bundle, but like most small businesses, the majority of owners work hard and get by.

- You need to do this because you enjoy providing people with good food. Most food truck owners love to use the phrase "you've got to taste this!" And they are passionate about what they create and serve.

- You need to wear many hats in this business from cook and server to marketer and promoter. Be as organized as possible.

- Don't get discouraged, even Kogi BBQ wasn't built in a day.

- Remember that following regulations, especially those set forth by the board of health are a pain in the neck, but they are at the root of your success.

- Spend a lot of time doing research. From looking for the best vehicle to finding the best locations to watching the Food Network for tasty ideas, do all sorts of research. It's actually fun if you are into the food truck culture.

- Treat customers, food providers, competitors, health inspectors, police officers with tickets in hand, angry storeowners, and everyone else you encounter along the way with respect. It can pay off well in the end.

- Have a sense of humor.

tip

Have someone with you to watch the buyers while you show them your van or truck. Believe it or not, opening up your truck to show someone around could lead to something being stolen.

Web advertising can be more costly, but placing a full-color ad on a website about the mobile food industry can be very effective. Again, be ready for callers or emails. In a web advertisement you can usually show a couple of photos as well as include more specific details about the equipment. Be accurate in whatever you write.

Appendix
Food Truck Resources

They say you can never be rich enough or thin enough. While these could be argued, we believe you can never have enough resources. Therefore, we're giving you a wealth of sources to check into, check out, and harness for your own personal information blitz.

These sources are tidbits—ideas to get you started on your research. They are by no means the only sources out there, and they should not be taken as the ultimate answer. We have done our research, but businesses do tend to move, change, fold, and expand. As we have repeatedly stressed, do your homework. Get out there and start investigating!

Agencies and Business Associations

Small Business Administration (SBA)
409 3rd Street
Washington, DC 20416
Phone: 800-827-5722
Website: sba.gov

▲

The U.S. Small Business Administration provides new entrepreneurs with a vast array of information on how to start and grow a business. It also has a business loans division that secures loans (but does not give them out). For more information on financing visit sba.gov/financing. To locate an SBA office in your region visit sba. gov/regions/states.html. You can also order the *U.S. SBA Small Business Startup Guide*.

United States Department of Labor
200 Constitution Avenue NW, Room C-2318
Washington, DC 20210
Phone: 866-4-USA-DOL
Website: dol.gov
Promotes opportunities for all kinds of small businesses and provides information on business laws, regulations, and wage information.

United State Patents and Trademarks Office
Commissioner for Patents
PO Box 1450
Alexandria, VA 22313-1450
Phone: 800-786-9199
Website: uspto.gov

The Internal Revenue Service (IRS)
Assistance and information for individuals: 800-829-1040
Assistance and information for businesses: 800-829-4933
Website: irs.gov
All the tax information you could possibly want from the source. Forms and information about filing are also available.

U.S. Chamber of Commerce
1615 H Street NW
Washington, DC 20062-2000
Phone: 202-659-6000
Customer Service: 800-638-6582
Website: uschamber.com
The U.S. Chamber of Commerce represents small businesses, corporations, and trade associations from coast to coast.

National Business Association
16775 Addison Road, Suite 410
Addison, Texas 75001
Phone: 800-456-0440
Website: nationalbusiness.org

A nonprofit association, the NBA can assist in helping small business owners team up to buy health plans, get educational opportunities, and secure other valuable services.

International Franchise Association (IFA)
1900 K Street, NW, Suite 700
Washington, DC 20006
Phone: 202-628-8000
Website: franchise.org
An association with a comprehensive website about franchising for both franchisers and franchisees.

U.S. Department of Health and Human Services
200 Independence Avenue SW
Washington, DC 20201
Phone: Toll Free: 1-877-696-6775
Website: hhs.gov/ or foodsafety.gov/index.html
The food safety section provides a wealth of information on health issues.

Centers for Disease Control and Prevention
1600 Clifton Rd.
Atlanta, GA 30329
Phone: 800-232-4636, TTY: 888-232-6348
Website: cdc.gov
On the CDC website you can find a map leading to all state departments of health.

Southern California Mobile Food Vendors Association
Phone: 424-229-2874
Website: socalmfva.com
Plenty of information for LA area mobile food entrepreneurs and others.

National Restaurant Association
2055 L Street NW, Suite 700
Washington, DC 20036
Phone: 202-331-5900
Website: restaurant.org
The mobile food industry is much like the restaurant business, only you have wheels and less overhead. You can find a lot of good information on a wide range of topics through the association's website.

National Association of Catering Executives
9891 Broken Land Parkway, Suite 301
Columbia, MD 21046
Phone: 410-290-5410
Website: nace.net

The oldest and largest catering association in the world, it encompasses all aspects of the catering industry.

The American Beverage Association
1101 16th St. NW
Washington, DC 20036
Phone: 202-463-6732
Website: ameribev.org
Founded in 1919 as the American Bottlers of Carbonated Beverages, today the ABA represents hundreds of beverage producers, distributors, franchise companies, and support industries.

American Culinary Federation
180 Center Place Way
St. Augustine, FL 32095
Phone: 904- 824-4468 or 800-624-9458
Website: acfchefs.org
Part of the American Culinary Foundation, founded in 1929, it now has over 200 chapters nationwide. When it comes to cooking, it is the expert.

Cart, Truck, Kiosk, Trailer, and Bus Designers and Manufacturers

Most of these companies will help you meet health compliance regulations in your city or state. Although some have "cart" in the name, many also sell kiosks.

800 Buy Cart
800buycart.com

All A Cart Manufacturing
allacart.com

Airstream Trailers
airstreamtrailers.com

All Star Carts and Kiosks
allstarcarts.com

American Mobile Kitchens LLC
americanmobilekitchens.com

Apollo Carts
apollocarts.com

California Cart Builder
californiacartbuilder.com

Carlin Manufacturing
carlinmfg.com

Cardinal Carts and Equipment. Inc.
cardinalcarts.com

Cart Concepts International
cartconcept.com

Cart-King
cart-king.com

CateringTruck.com™
cateringtruck.com

Concession Nation
consessionnation.com

Concession Trailers Warehouse
concessiontrailerswarehouse.com

Creative Mobile Systems
cmssystem.com

Custom Food Truck Builders
customfoodtruckbuilders.com

Custom Mobile Food Equipment
customsalesandservice.com

Festivals and Shows.com®
festivals-and-shows.com/catering-trucks-for-sale.html

Food Cart USA
foodcartusa.com

Food Trucks.org
foodtrucks.org

Food Trucks South
foodtruckssouth.com

Ice-Cream-Trucks.com
ice-cream-trucks.com

JJ Custom Built Food Trucks
jjcustombuiltfoodtrucks.com

Kareem Carts
kareemcarts.com (also a commissary in the Los Angeles area)

Kitchens on Wheels®
rollingkitchens.com

Legion Manufacturing
Legionmfg.com

M & R Specialty Trailers and Trucks
mr-trailers.com

Mobi Munch (food trucks)
mobimunch.com

MSM Catering Truck Manufacturing
msmcateringtrucks.com

Northwest Mobile Kitchens
northwestmobilekitchens.com

Prestige Food Trucks
prestigefoodtrucks.com

Roadstoves
roadstoves.com

Shanghai Mobile Kitchen Solutions
shanghaimks.com

Trovit (under cars section also has food lunch trucks)
cars.trovit.com/used-cars/catering-truck

U.S. Catering Trucks
uscateringtrucks.com

Used Vending
UsedVending.com

Vending Trucks.com
vendingtrucks.com

West Cost Catering Trucks
westcoastcateringtrucks.com

West Coast Custom Carts
westcoastcustomcarts.net

WYSS Catering Truck Manufacturing
wysscateringtrucks.com

Vehicle Wraps

Advertising Vehicles.com
advertisingvehicles.com

Cliff Digital
cliffdigital.com

San Diego vehicle wraps
sandiegovehiclewraps.com

Commercial Kitchens for Rent or Lease

BizKitchen
bizkitchens.com
Commercial kitchen postings and connections

Commercial Kitchens for Rent
commercialkitchenforrent.com
Kitchen rental state by state

Culinary Incubator Kitchens
culinaryincubator.com
Kitchen rental state by state

Chef's Kitchen (Los Angeles)
chefskitchens.com

Kitchen Chicago
kitchenchicago.com

The Kitchen Space (Austin)
thekitchenspace.com

La Cocina (San Francisco)
lacocinasf.org

WHEDco Kitchen Incubator (Bronx, NY)
whedco.org

Equipment and Supplies

Barbeques Galore
bbqgalore.com

Business.com
business.com

Directories of manufacturing companies, websites, and articles in various categories
Search under the following headings: beverages, bustaurants, trucks, food, kitchen equipment, food carts, food kiosks, food trailers, or food trucks.

The Fire Within . . .
firewithin.com (portable pizza ovens)

Food Service Warehouse
foodservicewarehouse.com
Tons of equipment at your fingertips

My Cleaning Products
mycleaningproducts.com
Natural cleaning products

Northern Pizza Equipment Inc.
northernpizzaequipment.com

Franchising

Entrepreneur Top 500 Franchises
entrepreneur.com/franchise500/index.html

Franchise Business Review
franchisebusinessreview.com
Comprehensive publication about franchising

Franchise Gator
franchisegator.com

International Franchise Association (IFA)
franchise.org

Funding

Eco Business Links
ecobusinesslinks.com/green_venture_capital
Green business investors

Funding Post
fundingpost.com
Runs venture capital and angel showcases nationwide where entrepreneurs can meet with VCs and angels to discuss funding new projects (such as your mobile food business)

Go 4 Funding

go4funding.com/articles/angel-investors/angel-investor-network.aspx

Listing of angel investors and their websites.

Indiegogo

indiegogo.com

Crowd funding site that claims to be open for funding anything. Watch the fees.

Micro Ventures

microventures.com

Venture Capital style investing on a smaller level

Mobile Food Industry Information

Buzzle.com Food and Drink

buzzle.com/chapters/food-and-drink.asp

Food articles and plenty of recipes

HotDogBiz101.com

hotdogbiz101.com

All about owning a hot dog cart

Find LA Food Trucks

findlafoodtrucks.com

Locations plus blogs and other information about LA food trucks

FoodTrucksIn.com

foodtrucksin.com

Food truck locations, blogs, reports, and soon to add help finding anything from fresh organic food to a spare tire.

Midtown Lunch

midtownlunch.com

Data about the mobile food business in several cities

Mobile Catering Business.com

mobilecateringbusiness.com

Links to articles, business plans, forums, books, and more

Mobile Food News

mobilefoodnews.com

News and information about the mobile food industry

New York Street Food

newyorkstreetfood.com

The latest updates on the NY street food scene

Sally's Place
sallybernstein.com/food/chefs-corner/organizations.htm
Includes a long listing of professional food organizations, articles, and more

National Food Suppliers and Food Clubs' Websites

BJs
bjs.com

Cheney Brothers (South East)
cheneybrothers.com

Costco
costco.com

Food and Beverage Network
foodandbeverage-network.com

Food Service.com
foodservice.com

Jetro
jetro.com

National Food Exchange
nationalfoodexchange.com

Natural Food Co-ops
coopdirectory.org

Performance Food Group
pfgc.com

Convenience Foods

Restaurant Depot
restaurantdepot.com
For people in the restaurant and food business like you.

Sam's Club
samsclub.com

Smart and Final (West Coast)
smartandfinal.com

Sysco
sysco.com

United Natural Foods
unfi.com

US Foodservice
usfoodservice.com

Catering Supplies

Catering Supplies.com
cateringsupplies.com

A S Catering Supplies, Ltd.
ascateringsupplies.com
Numerous supplies and a newsletter

Other Business Websites

Business Plans

Bplans.com
bplans.com
Expert advice, business planning tools, and sample business plans

BizPlanDB
bizplan.com
Online business plan software

Credit Bureaus

Equifax
800-685-1111
equifax.com

Experian
888-397-3742
experian.com

TransUnion
transunion.com

Incorporation and Legal

The Company Corporation
incorporate.com

Nolo.com
nolo.com

USAGov.com
usa.gov/Business/Incorporate.shtml
U.S. government's official website included data on incorporating in all 50 states

Business Books

55 Surefire Food-Related Businesses You Can Start for Under $5,000, Entrepreneur Press and Cheryl Kimball, Irvine, CA: Entrepreneur Press, 2009.

Food Truck Road Trip—A Cookbook: More Than 100 Recipes Collected from the Best Street Food Vendors Coast to Coast Paperback, Kim Pham, Philip Shen and Terri Phillips, Salem, MA: Page Street Publishing, 2014

The Food Truck Handbook: Start, Grow, and Succeed in the Mobile Food Business, David Webber, Indianapolis, IN: Wiley and Sons, 2012

Food Trucks: Dispatches and Recipes from the Best Kitchens on Wheels, Heather Shouse, Berkeley, CA: Ten Speed Press, 2011

From Kitchen to Market: Selling Your Gourmet Food Specialty, Stephen Hall, Chicago: Kaplan Business, 2005.

Write Your Business Plan: Get Your Plan in Place and Your Business off the Ground, The Staff of Entrepreneur Media, Inc., Irvine, CA: Entrepreneur, 2014.

Small Business Software

Business software can help you with bookkeeping, record keeping, vendor and supplier lists, paying taxes, etc.

Business Plan Pro and Palo Alto Software Marketing Plan Pro
paloalto.com

QuickBooks Pro 2015
quickbooks.Intuit.com

Quicken Deluxe 2015
quicken.Intuit.com

Internet Business Resources

All Business
> allbusiness.com

Articles, information, tips, links, business forms, directories, expert commentary, etc.

Cafepress.com
> cafepress.com

Helps you sell gifts and promotional products from your website

Entrepreneur Online
> entrpreneur.com

Articles, information, tips, links, business forms, directories, expert commentary, etc.

Go Daddy
> godaddy.com

For building your website

MerchantProExpress.com
> merchantproexpress.com

Provides merchant accounts and credit card processing options and solutions

Network Solutions
> networksolutions.com

Helps you search for web domain names

Nolo.com
> nolo.com

Comprehensive legal site with listings of attorneys in your state, plus articles, legal
forms, and much more

Thomas Register
> thomasnet.com

Helps you search for registered and unregistered trademark names

Additional Online Resources and Recipe Websites

Abouteating.com

Allrecipes.com

Americastestkitchen.com

Bbc.co.uk/food/recipes

Bestfoods.com

Betterrecipes.com

BettyCrocker.com

Campbellsoup.com

CDkitchen.com

Chinavista.com/culture/cuisine/recipes.html

Cook123.com

Cooking.com

Cookingcache.com

Cookingconnect.com (cooking appliance reviews)

Cooks.com

Culinarybusiness.com

Epicurious.com (recipes)

Food.com

Foodnetwork.com

Healthrecipes.com

Ihirechefs.com (chef hiring website)

KatenConsulting.com (food serving etiquette and training)

Mobilecravings.com (food truck index in many states)

Myrecipes.com

Onestopcandle.com (chocolate and candy-making supply company)

Recipes2.alastra.com

Thefruitpages.com

Whatscookingamerica.net

Whfoods.com

Glossary

AirPot beverage dispenser: A thermal beverage holder that uses vacuum insulation to keep contents hot or cold. It uses air to pump out the contents, so it is referred to as an "air" pot.

Background check: The process of looking up and compiling data on a potential employee, such as a criminal past or work-related inconsistencies with information provided.

Brand: The identity of a product, service, or business, which can include the name, logo, slogan, or anything else unique to the business.

Business plan: A detailed plan of how the business will be started, operated, and will show a profit. Business plans are divided into several sections and tell the story of the business particularly (but not exclusively) for potential financial backers.

▲

Business summary: A short version of a business plan that tells the key points of how the business will operate and earn money. Can also be incorporated into a PowerPoint presentation.

Cold trays: Thermal trays that when heated work like a freezer to store cold foods or beverages.

Commercial kitchen: A kitchen owned and operated to be rented out commercially for use by others.

Commercial line of credit: Not unlike a credit card, it is a line of credit extended by a bank or credit bureau specifically to a business.

Commissary kitchen: Another name for a commercial kitchen.

Convection oven: An oven using a fan to shorten the cooking time by circulating hot air uniformly around the food.

Credit reports: A detailed report of an individual's credit history prepared by a credit bureau and used by a lender to determine a loan applicant's creditworthiness.

Credit union: A cooperative organization that makes loans to its members at low interest rates.

DBA (Doing Business As): Name used for business purposes that is not the legal name of the individual or organization actually conducting the business. The DBA is typically on file at the courthouse as a fictitious name by which you or your company does business.

Employer Identification Number or EIN (aka a federal tax ID): According to the IRS, it is also known as a Federal Tax Identification Number and is used to identify a business entity. Generally, businesses need an EIN.

Fire-suppression device: An automatic warning and shut-down device attached to an oven or stove to shut it down in the event of a fire.

Flattop grill: A grill resembling a griddle, except the heating element is circular rather than straight.

Foot traffic: Pedestrians who pass your location.

Franchise: An agreement between a company franchising its business model to business owners who agree to operate a business according to the rules and regulations of the franchising company.

Franchisee: The buyer/owner of an individual franchise or several franchises from a franchising company.

Franchisor: The company selling a franchise.

Gross vehicle weight: What a vehicle weighs at any given time.

Hood/commercial hood: A hood captures all contamination from grease and oil emanating from a stove or grill. It must be removed and cleaned periodically.

POS technology: Point-of-sale (POS) technology calculates items checked out using computer software.

Propane tank: A tank, often used on food trucks, that contains the colorless gas C3H8 (found in natural gas and petroleum) and widely used as a source of energy for onboard equipment.

Pushcarts: A light cart pushed by hand.

Retrofit: To remodel, design, and/or refurbish a cart, truck, trailer, kiosk, or bus to meet the needs of the owner.

Serving windows: The window on the side of the vehicle through which orders are taken and customers are served.

Social media: The various forms of online communication including blogs and social media platforms such as Twitter, Facebook, Foursquare, and Instagram.

Transparency: In business, it means making the systems, policies, operating procedures, and financial data (within reason) available to shareholders and the public.

Viral marketing: Online marketing that replicates word-of-mouth marketing. Viral refers to the speed of spreading the word (it is not a negative term such as a virus). Forwarding to a friend or a specific message at the end of a mass email can be forms of viral marketing.

Zoning: A municipality's way of dividing up a territory (city, town, etc.) by commercial and residential areas.

Index